Tholsel 1861   KC, GD

Dedicated to Mary Balfe

John's Bridge 1861 KC

KILKENNY

Its Architecture & History

Edited by
Katherine M Lanigan
& Gerald Tyler
assisted by
Margery Brady

Appletree Press

Published and printed by The Appletree Press Ltd, 7 James Street South, Belfast BT2 8DL. This edition first published and distributed in Britain 1987

Designed by Richard Eckersley at Kilkenny Design Workshops, Kilkenny

Cover illustration: Kilkenny, probably late 17th century, artist unknown (courtesy National Library of Ireland)

Proceeds from the sale of this book will be given to the new Kilkenny Theatre and similar Kilkenny restoration funds.

Kilkenny Castle 1861   KC, GD

Second edition
© An Taisce, Kilkenny Association, 1977, 1986. All rights reserved. No part of this publication may be reproduced, stored in a retrieval system or transmitted in any form or by any means, electronic, mechanical, photocopying, recording or otherwise, without the permission of the copyright owner.

British Library Cataloguing in Publication Data
Kilkenny : its architecture & history.
—2nd ed.
1. Architecture—Ireland—Kilkenny (Kilkenny)—History
I. Lanigan, Katherine M. II. Tyler, Gerald
III. Brady, Margery
720'.9418'9   NA991.K54

ISBN 0-86281-180-5

9 8 7 6 5 4 3 2 1

Contents

6 Preface

9 A General Historical Outline

Section 1
Buildings of National, Historical and Architectural Importance

19 Kilkenny Castle
21 Shee Alms House
23 St Mary's Church and Graveyard
24 Rothe House
26 St Francis Abbey
27 The Black Abbey
28 St Canice's Cathedral
30 St Canice's Library
31 The Bishop's Palace
32 The Priory of St John the Evangelist

Section 2
The Character of Kilkenny

35 Kenny's Well
36 Talbot's Castle and the City Wall
36 The Slips
38 Tudor Kilkenny
39 Georgian Kilkenny
42 Kilkenny Writers

Section 3
The Streets of Kilkenny

47 The Parade
49 Castle Road
50 Patrick Street
53 Ormonde Road
54 College Road
55 Rose Inn Street
58 Horseleap Slip
59 Canal Walk
59 High Street
68 Friary Street
68 Pennefeather Lane
69 William Street
70 Chapel Lane and Wellington Square
72 James Street
73 James Sconce
73 Evans Lane
74 James Green
75 Parnell Street
75 St Mary's Lane
76 St Kieran's Street
79 Parliament Street
84 Watergate
85 Irishtown
86 Dean Street
87 Butts Green
87 Friar's Bridge Street
88 Blackmill Street
89 Coach Road and Church Lane
89 Loreto View
90 St Canice's Place
90 Velvet Lane and St Canice's Steps
91 Vicar Street
91 Common Hill Lane
91 Troy's Gate
92 Green Street
92 John's Quay
94 John Street Lower
98 Maudlin Street
99 Michael Street
100 John Street Upper
101 Dublin Road
102 John's Green
102 Barrack Street
102 Wolfe Tone Street
102 Castlecomer Road
102 Hebron Road

104 Architectural Glossary

110 Bibliographical References

Index to Buildings of Importance and Streets
(inside back cover)

Preface to Second Edition

Few changes have been made to the text of our first edition of 1977 although some photographs have been replaced. However, many changes have occurred on the streets of Kilkenny, and most of these are for the better, especially shopfronts and street furniture. Two major buildings, Rothe House and Shee Alms House have been further restored. The Tholsel is returning to its former glory after a tragic fire in 1985. Our Local Authorities have received national and international awards for urban renewal of derelict areas in Maudlin Street and Dean Street, and the new Ring Road alleviates traffic in the city centre.

Most of our helpers are still with us but Mary Balfe, an enthusiastic worker, alas died in 1978. Richard Ekersley has left us for the United States where we wish him well. He has agreed to some minor changes in design. The additional short index will hopefully make it easier to find a particular site or street.

This edition was co-ordinated by Margery Brady under the direction of editors Gerald Tyler and Katherine Lanigan.

The following undertook research, wrote articles or gave advice:
Mary Balfe, Dorcas Birthistle, Adrian Bligh, John Bradley, Margery Brady, Brendan Conway, Maurice Craig DA (Edin) ARIBA, Thomas G Crotty, Peter Smithwick, Anna DeLoughry, Richard Eckersley, Sally FitzMaurice, Maureen Hegarty, Mary Kenealy, Andrew Lane, Katherine M Lanigan, W Percy Le Clerc, MRIAI, ARIBA, Tom Lyng, The Right Reverend Henry McAdoo, Bishop of Ossory, Frank McEvoy, Edward McParland, Trinity College, Mary Mullen, Colm O'Cochlain, BArch, Eamon O'Doherty, MRIA, Jim Horan, Don Cromer, Dennis Bannister, Margaret M Phelan, Don Roberts, Gerald Tyler, Bill Walsh.

Some of the definitions in the Architechtural Glossary are by courtesy of An Foras Forbartha.

We are grateful to the following for permission to reproduce drawings, photographs and maps. Illustrations are attributed in the captions by the following initials:

KC, The President St Kieran's College for drawings from a plan of the city of Kilkenny 1861 Marlow Brothers Dublin: AP, Annamult Prints: NG, The National Gallery of Ireland: BS, The Butler Society: BF, Bord Failte Eireann: IT, Irish Times: EOD, Eamon O'Doherty: O, Oliver, Photographer, Kilkenny: NM, National Museum of Ireland: CPW, Commisioners of Public Works in Ireland: TB, Tom Brett, Photographer, Kilkenny: BA, Community of Black Abbey: PDI, D.H. Davison and John Hunt: MF, Mark Fiennes, photographer, Kilkenny: GT, Gerald Tyler: GD, Gerry Deegan, photographer, Kilkenny: NL, The National Library of Ireland: COC, Colm O'Cochlain, Kilkenny: ROC, Richard O'Carroll, Kilkenny: OS, Ordnance Survey, Dublin: MP, Lady M Ponsonby: MQ, Michael Quinn: KB, Kevin Boyle.

Katherine Lanigan was born in Kilkenny. Her parents' families, Harte and Birch, were long settled there so she was introduced at an early age to the lore of the City and County.

Educated in Ireland and France she graduated from University College, Dublin in 1934.

A founder-member of Kilkenny Archaeological Society, Mrs Lanigan is Honorary Curator of Rothe House Museum. She has written short histories of Kilkenny Castle and Rothe House and has contributed articles on local history to 'The Old Kilkenny Review', 'The Journal of the Butler Society', and 'Ireland of the Welcomes'.

Gerald Tyler, Manager of Information at Kilkenny Design, was born in Yorkshire and has lived in Kilkenny since 1969. At times during this period he has been a member of the National Executive of An Taisce (the National Trust for Ireland), the management committee of the Irish Agricultural Museum and the Society of Designers in Ireland; a Director of the Crafts Council of Ireland; Chairman of the Irish Country Furniture Society and Kilkenny Arts Week. He has made a study of traditional rural crafts and has lectured and written articles on the subject.

The Cathedral 1861, KC

Detail 14th century tomb, St Canice's AP

General Historical Outline

The Pre-Norman Settlement

The 'faire Kilkenny' of Edmund Spenser's poem has also been called 'The Marble City' from its abundance of black limestone. It is essentially a mediaeval town of the thirteenth century; a product of the Norman conquest. But the round tower which stands by its Cathedral tells us that the Cill Chainnig was there before the Normans ever set foot in Ireland. We know, too, from excavation, that a Romanesque Church of the twelfth century was torn down to build the Cathedral indicating that the settlement there was one of substance. St. Cainneach, who founded it, died in 599. His monastic town must have had a span of about six centuries before Strongbow and his men took over.
Mac Giolla Phadraig, Chieftain of Ossory was defeated by the first wave of Norman invaders and Strongbow who arrived in 1170 was able to occupy the natural fortress at the bend of the river (where now stands Kilkenny Castle).

Mediaeval Kilkenny

Mediaeval Kilkenny was a conception of the Norman mind. While Strongbow fortified the castle site before his death in 1176, the main organisation of the town fell to his successor, William the Earl Marshall and his five sons.

In spite of the undoubted religious scholarship of earlier centuries the Normans were not impressed by the quality of the Christianity they found in 1169 and their religious foundations doubtless aimed at the education of the native population in their Christian values.

A magnificent spate of building from about 1200 to 1245 resulted in a fortified settlement with three monasteries, a cathedral, a parish church and a strong castle. Such a programme of construction in so short a time could not have been achieved without the help of a larger labour force than the Normans appear to have brought with them. One supposes, therefore, that the native community played a considerable part in the achievement and that they continued to live in the area around the new Cathedral (still known as Irishtown) which was under ecclesiastical rule.

The Normans fortified for themselves the area between the Castle and the junction of the Nore and Bregagh rivers. This walled town was quite small but it included the castle, the parish church of St. Mary's and one monastery, the Abbey of St Francis (the Grey Friars).

The other monasteries, the Abbey of the Holy Trinity, under the Rule of St Dominic (Black Friars), in Irishtown and the Priory of St John the Evangelist (Augustinian) across the river were outside the walls.

The Rise of the Feudal Families

William, the Earl Marshall, gave Kilkenny its first charter about 1207. It was not directly under the crown but was governed by a Sovereign, or Chief Officer, and burgesses with a Council of Twelve who had the power of legislation and taxation.

College 1861   KC, GD

The protection thus given to trade and commerce facilitated the rise to power and affluence of a number of Anglo-Norman families who soon seized power and by a system of close intermarriage retained it for many centuries. These leading families, ten in number were Archdekin, Archer, Cowley, Langton, Lee, Knaresborough, Lawless, Ragget, Rothe and Shee. All except Shee were of Anglo-Norman origin. They contibuted a great deal to the establishment of an orderly, prosperous and well planned town just as their counterparts did in the English town of Galway. In both towns they were supplanted by the Cromwellian settlers who derisively referred to the Galway families as *tribes*.

The Kyteler Case

The relative tranquillity of this thriving market town was rudely shattered in 1324 by an event which was to have repercussions throughout English-occupied Ireland. The full story of the Kyteler Witchcraft Case has not come down to us but it appears to have been a major revolt against church authority.

Alice Kyteler was born about 1280 into a Norman-French family long settled in Kilkenny. Her father was a Banker or money-lender, a business which Alice continued to pursue with success and which she passed on to a son — one of several children. Her husbands, four in number, all belonged to distinguished Norman families — Outlaw, Le Blond (White), de Valle (Wall), and Le Poer (Power). Her profession of money-lending, though disapproved of by the Church brought her great wealth. It is not surprising, therefore, that her trial for heresy and sorcery built up into a major struggle to uphold the discipline of the Church; or that the proceedings occupied nine months of the year 1324; or that Alice succeeded in escaping punishment in the end by fleeing the country.

Heresy, witchcraft and sorcery were common expressions of revolt against Church authority throughout Europe at the time but the contemporary narrative records that such things were unknown in Ireland.

Alice's antagonist was Richard de Ledrede, Bishop of Ossory. An English Franciscan monk, de Ledrede had been appointed to Ossory by Pope John XXII in 1318, the incumbent being promoted to Cashel to make room for him. It is likely that he was sent specially to deal with the situation. The senechal of Kilkenny, Arnold le Poer and other friends of Kyteler were, at this time, sufficiently hibernicised to resent the interference of an Englishman and Le Poer went so far as to imprison the Bishop in Kilkenny Castle. The power of the Church prevailed. Convictions were secured against Alice, her son William Outlaw and ten of her followers, of whom one Petronilla of Meath was burned at the stake. Le Poer, the Senechal, died in prison, Kyteler escaped to Scotland and the revolt was quelled. Bishop de Ledrede, himself, was faced with a charge of heresy and, rather than face trial, fled to the Papal Court of Avignon where he remained for twenty years.

Detail of tomb, 1557, St Canice's AP

Statutes of Kilkenny

The hibernicisation of the English Settlers already referred to began to worry the Crown during the reign of Edward III. A Parliament held at Kilkenny in 1366 enacted the notorious Statutes of Kilkenny designed to enforce rigid segregation of the Anglo-Norman settlers from the native Irish population. Intermarriage, adoption of the Irish language or customs were equated with high treason. The Statutes were unsuccessful but did create something of a cleavage between the races and prepared the way for later strife.

The Butlers

In 1391 an event occurred which was crucial to the future of Kilkenny. The Castle was purchased from the descendants of William (the Earl Marshall) by James Butler, 3rd Earl of Ormonde.

The Butlers were first and always King's men. Arriving in Ireland in the retinue of Henry II they were rewarded by him with large grants of land and with the Chief Butlership of Ireland — an honour which carried considerable material benefit. Royal patronage was cemented by a marriage with the granddaughter of Edward II in the early 14th century. King Richard II was the first of many monarchs to visit the Butlers at Kilkenny Castle. In spite of several quarrels with the monarchy they retained the King's confidence for the five and a half centuries which they spent in the Castle and frequently acted as his Deputy. Being closely inter-married with the Irish chieftains they were able to act as go-between in disputes with the English establishment. The 3rd Earl, for example, was a fluent Irish speaker in spite of the Statutes of Kilkenny. The City exerted considerable influence on national affairs through the Butlers.

The Reformation

There is no recorded protest against the closure of Kilkenny's monasteries under Henry VIII. Their property in the city passed to the civic authorities. The impact of the reformation was minimal until 1553, when an Englishman named John Bale, a fanatical reformer, was appointed Bishop of Ossory. A former Carmelite Friar, he was a scholar of some note with several works to his credit. His career in Kilkenny was short but lively. He did considerable damage to the Cathedral by breaking statues and images but on the credit side he organised the citizens to act morality plays (written by himself) at the Market Cross which formerly stood near the present Tholsel. His mission was a failure and he was driven out by popular anger, his life being saved by the intervention of the "Sovereign and his troop".

The pressure of the reformers continued as a harassment which varied in intensity but which in time led to rebellion and to the formation of the Confederation of Kilkenny.

The Confederation of Kilkenny

The period from 1580 to 1648 was a prosperous one for the city. Black Tom, 10th Earl of Ormonde was the trusted friend of Queen Elizabeth and his influence protected the town from the depredations associated with the Elizabethan re-conquest. His support of the crown was rewarded by a Royal Charter of James I in 1609 constituting Kilkenny as a city. The Sovereign and Council of Twelve were replaced by a Mayor, Aldermen and Councillors.

Following the Ulster Rebellion of 1641 a Confederacy was set up to unite Catholics of English and Irish extraction in defence of their common faith, their

Detail Rothe Monument, St Canice's 1642 AP

rights and liberties. Kilkenny was selected as the centre for the National Parliament. Buildings such as Rothe House, the Shee House in Parliament Street (now removed) and Kilkenny Castle were useful for the meetings of Parliament, of the Supreme Council and of the Bishops and Clergy.

David Rothe, Bishop of Ossory, took a leading part. The Confederation sat for six years 1642 — 1648 and governed the country during a period of extreme turmoil. The civil conflict between King and Parliament was complicated by the extreme bitterness of the religious war in Ireland. Political moves for peace were carried on between two members of the Butler family, the Lord Viscount Mountgarrett (President of the Supreme Council of the Confederation) and James, Marquess of Ormonde (later Duke), who acted for the King. The situation was further complicated by the advent of John Baptist Rinuccini as Papal Nuncio to the Confederation in 1645. Rinuccini brought arms and money for the Catholic cause and was received with great pomp and much rejoicing in Kilkenny Castle. He had little understanding, however, of the delicacy of the Irish situation. He opposed all efforts for peace, alienated the Bishops, and broke the solidarity of the Confederation.

The Parliament brought considerable prosperity to Kilkenny as is evidenced by many elaborate tombstones of the period in the city churches and grave yards.

Cromwell in Kilkenny

Cromwell's attack on Kilkenny came in March 1650. He found a town disheartened by the failure of its Parliament, wearied by war and dissension, and ravaged by plague. Colonel Walter Butler repulsed him from the Castle Gate but by circling the town he breached the wall near the Franciscan monastery and forced the surrender of the garrison.

His soldiers were let loose in St. Canice's Cathedral where much damage was done to sculptured monuments and stained-glass windows. The worst blow to the citizens was the wholesale confiscation of property. Most of the leading citizens had been involved in the Confederation and so were marked men. However, many of those who were banished to Connaught failed to claim the land assigned to them there preferring to hang on without legal right in Kilkenny and on the restoration of King Charles in 1660, the Duke of Ormonde, as Viceroy, was able to secure the return of some of the citizens' property. He

Detail Rothe Monument, St Canice's 1642 AP

rebuilt the Castle, established a school and restored some confidence to the citizens. Yet the Cromwellian confiscations marked the end of the era of the Anglo-Norman city. By 1700 the Williamite confiscations had sealed the fate of the Catholic Anglo-Irish and from thence those who failed to find a place in the armies of France and Spain made common cause with, and became indistinguishable from the native Irish. Property and wealth passed to new owners and the Rothes, Shees and Archers faded into obscurity.

James II, during his short reign interested himself in Kilkenny. He gave the city a new Charter and established the University of St Canice in Kilkenny College, but the Battle of the Boyne and the flight of James put an end to this six-months-old foundation.

The 18th Century

Records are sparse for early 18th century. The Penal Laws against Catholics became effective quite soon after 1700. Control of civic offices passed to the Protestants and new English names such as Haydock, Warren, etc. replaced those of traditional Kilkenny 'tribes'.

The newcomers, still insecure, initiated few changes. For the Catholics, secrecy was the key to survival. Their activities are not recorded. Moreover, education for them could only be secured through contacts with emigrant members of the old civic families who had fled to continental Europe after 1690, and of course, through 'hedge' schools.

An abortive Jacobite plot in 1715 (recorded in Corporation Documents) was quickly suppressed and resulted in the unseating of the Mayor, a secret Papist.

St Kieran's College 1861 KC

Kilkenny did not recover from this trauma until well into the second half of the century. Most of the Georgian buildings which remain, such as the Tholsel, Kilkenny College, the Kilkenny Design Workshops (Castle Stables) were built from 1760 onwards. Catholic education emerged from the shadows with the founding of St Kieran's College in 1782.

The gloom of this dark century was compounded by the eclipse of the Ormonde family in 1715. The flight of the second Duke of Ormonde from a charge of treason left the Castle unoccupied for 50 years. When the Butlers were re-instated towards the end of the century the new landowners surrounding the city had also regained confidence and began to make a contribution to the life of the community. The big house tradition spilled into the city and gave rise, first to a revival of gaiety, expressed in activities of the Inns and Taverns such as the 'Hole in the Wall' and the strolling players who began to perform regularly in the Tholsel. The 'diversions' of the country house tradition blossomed into a full scale cultural revival in the following century.

The 19th Century

The Kilkenny Private Theatre of 1802-1819 was inspired by the 18th century tradition of country house amateur theatricals. It was closely associated with the Kilkenny Hunt and both ventures originated with the brothers Richard and John Power of Kilfane. Centred in the City, they proved successful.

Apart from increased trade and the stimulation of numerous distinguished foreign visitors, the city benefited by being involved in the sporting and cultural activity of the surrounding countryside, an involvement which was to outlast the theatre.

It was the encouragement of Tom Moore, one of the Theatre's actors, for example, which inspired John Banim to take up a literary career and his brother Michael earned his living by selling sports goods to the gentry.

Mid-century saw the rise of the numerous small cultural societies — literary, scientific, historical, archaeological, which have been a feature of the town to the present day. The most enduring of these was the Kilkenny Archaeological Society founded by Reverend James Graves and John G. Prim in 1849. After a successful career of fifty years in Kilkenny it was transferred to Dublin and became the Royal Society of Antiquaries of Ireland.

The end of the century saw the 'All Ireland Literary Review' produced by Standish O'Grady, Editor of Kilkenny Moderator, and a revival of theatrical endeavour under Captain Cuffe and the Countess of Desart in association with the Gaelic League.

Despite its cultural brilliance the 19th century was not a prosperous one for Kilkenny. Yet there is the fine Catholic Cathedral of St Mary's built, incredibly, during the Famine period, two other Catholic Churches and some excellent cut-stone buildings such as the Bank of Ireland, the Provincial Bank and the

St Mary's Cathedral, 1861 KC

Presbyterian Church. Perhaps the best that can be said of the period of the union as far as Kilkenny is concerned is that the city retained more of its interesting ancient architecture than if it had been wealthier.

The 20th Century

It is pleasant to note that in the present century the city, while spreading and developing rapidly, retains its cultural tradition.

An Art Gallery Society was formed in 1943 to provide the City with its own collection of modern paintings. This collection is being installed in the Castle.

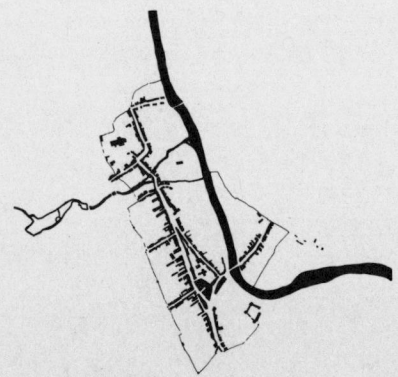

Kilkenny c. 1280

The second Kilkenny Archaeological Society was founded in 1945 and the Kilkenny Arts Society in 1952. Drama was provided by Ossory Players and presently by the New Theatre Group, but alas, without a permanent theatre. In the decade 1960 to 1970 Kilkenny Literary Society published eighteen issues of 'The Kilkenny Magazine'. August 1974 saw the launching of a very successful annual Arts Week, a festival which includes music, poetry and the visual arts. The most generous gift of the present century to Kilkenny was made by the 6th Marquess of Ormonde in 1967. He gave Kilkenny Castle to the Citizens and its park to the Nation. When the building is fully restored it will supply some of the needs which arise from Kilkenny's literary and artistic tradition — in particular an art gallery and a theatre.

Kilkenny Design Workshops in the former Castle stables has had a vital influence on the artistic life of the city. Craftsmen trained in silver and ceramic work by the Workshop have remained in the area to carry on their work. The coming and going of foreign artists again revivifies the old town lest it sink into slumber under the weight of its history.

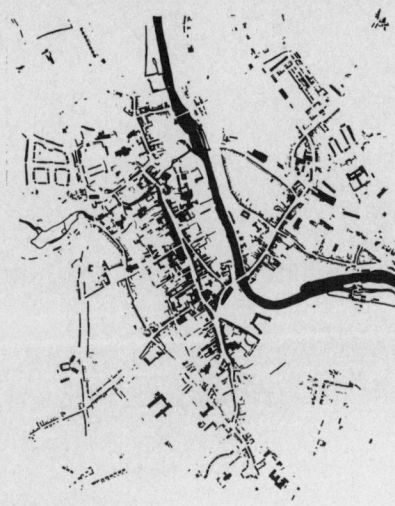

Kilkenny c. 1946

The Museum provided by the Kilkenny Archaeological Society in the sixteenth century Rothe House makes a valuable educational and artistic centre.

To understand Kilkenny's unique character one should retire from the busy streets to the lovely Castle Park and, standing within the shadow of the ancient pile, contemplate the great jumble of roof-tops, old and young, which tumble down to the quiet-flowing river beneath. Here dove-grey spires and battlemented towers proclaim a city old in Christian living and wise in human experience. One can feel the heartbeat of an ancient civilized community.

1
Buildings of National, Historical and Architectural Importance

The Castle from John's Bridge BF

First Duke of Ormonde by Lely NG

Second Duke of Ormonde by Kneller NG

KILKENNY CASTLE

Kilkenny Castle stands on a magnificent site on the southern extremity of the town. A natural stronghold, it overlooks the two fords of the Nore (now furnished with bridges) and the entire Norman town. Beneath its walls the river bends eastward for half a mile before resuming its southward course.

The first defences thrown up by Strongbow were probably earthen. The building of the stone fortress fell to his successor William, the Earl Marshall. The enclosing walls were begun about 1195 and the Castle itself in the early years of the 13th century. It can boast of 700 years of continuous occupation and, of course, of frequent rebuilding and repair.

Ownership passed, by purchase, from the descendants of William Marshall to the Butlers, Earls of Ormonde in 1391. This influential Norman family had earlier contracted a royal alliance and throughout most of their long career in Kilkenny they enjoyed the royal favour, frequently acting as King's Deputy or Viceroy. Equally, alliances with the Gaelic royal family of Leinster, the McMurrough Kavanaghs and with those of other Gaelic chieftains enabled them to negotiate successfully with the latter during the troubled period of the later Middle Ages. Hence Kilkenny and its castle played a major part in the history of that part of Ireland controlled by the Normans. The stability of the Butler seat is well exemplified in the mass of records relating to many families, Gaelic and Norman, which were deposited there. These were preserved intact until 1947 when they were transferred to the National Library of Ireland. They provide a most valuable collection of historical source material for the nation.

During the Confederation 1642—48 the Castle was in the hands of a Catholic Branch of the Butlers (Mountgarrett) and was used for the administration of the Confederacy and for the reception of dignataries such as the Papal Nuncio, Rinuccini.

The building received a severe battering on the South side from the Cromwellian army which attacked it in 1650. The attackers found it too formidable a fortress and retired, eventually gaining entry to the city at another point.

On the restoration of Charles II in 1660, the Castle reverted again to the major branch of the family. The King rewarded the 12th Earl for his considerable services to the Monarchy in exile by creating him 1st Duke of Ormonde. Thereafter followed a brilliant period for the Castle. It was rebuilt in the French style and handsome gardens laid out. These have recently been restored and some of the statuary has been replaced.

Restoration was continued by the 2nd Duke who built the great gate early in the 18th century. But the period of affluence came to an abrupt end in 1715 when the Duke was impeached for involvement in a Jacobite plot and fled to France rather than face the charge.

He forfeited all honours and titles but the Castle was permitted to remain in the caretaker hands of his brother for the next 50 years.

Towards the end of the 18th century honours and titles other than the Dukedom were restored to the Butlers and restoration of the Castle quickly followed. The family continued to enjoy the Royal favour and early in the 19th century received a Marquessate.

They had long enjoyed the privilege of exacting prisage of wines at the ports of Ireland. In 1810 this privilege was surrendered to the Crown for a compensation figure of £216,000. A major reconstruction of the Castle was initiated. This, with further additions about 1860 constitutes the present building.

The Butlers vacated Kilkenny Castle in 1936 and in 1967 the 6th Marquess (24th Earl) presented it to the citizens of Kilkenny. At the same time the gardens and parkland were given to the Nation. The National Park was quickly opened to the public and work has begun on the restoration of the Castle buildings with the East wing being opened to the public in 1976.

This 13th century castle was restored or rebuilt at least four times but on no occasion was it completely demolished except, perhaps, the east wing, so that the present very pleasing neo-gothic structure has an individuality denied to many of the gothic revival castles of Ireland.

The original wedge-shaped four-towered fortress plan has been preserved throughout, although the castle now lacks its south eastern tower and its southern curtain wall with central gateway.

The most spectacular of the earlier re-constructions was that of the first Duke in 1680-87. It excited the admiration of many visitors of the period and was said to have been inspired by French castles which the Duke had studied during his exile with Charles II. It was probably the work of Sir William Robinson, the Surveyor-General, who had built for the Duke the Royal Hospital, Kilmainham, and the Ormonde residence at Chapelizod.

A 'rescue' operation by the 16th Earl around 1780 (after the caretaker period) was largely obscured by the totally different concept which 19th century architects brought to castle architecture.

In 1826-37 a major reconstruction was carried out by William Robertson (see page 54, Rosehill) which radically altered the appearance of the castle. The present north block and west wing are his work. Robertson represents the earliest school of mediaeval revivalists of the 19th century tradition. For example he retained the early 18th century classical gateway in the west wall and added Adamesque swags to it. The stepped battlement of the chimneys of the Duke's castle were replaced by a continuous battlement — the Towers were raised and ornamented with crenellations and mock machicolations. A slender flag tower added behind the north-eastern tower gives a pleasing asymmetric appearance to the building.

Robertson had to rebuild the south facade of the main north block. He enlarged the windows and added a gallery on the ground floor.

To him or his sculptor must be attributed the very fine sculptured heads in the classical manner which appear on this gallery and on the new doorway of the south tower. The rainwater heads with their ducal coronet and date 1682 survive from the ducal castle.

The eastern wing containing the impressive picture gallery was designed by Benjamin Woodward of the Cork firm of Deane and Woodward 1860-62. Woodward, a brilliant architect and close friend of Ruskin, was strongly influenced by Italian ideas and specialized in Venetian Gothic. He died at an early age in 1861 before the Kilkenny work was finished. The Engineering School in Trinity College and the Kildare Street

Sixth Marquess of Ormonde MP

The Harrison Chimney Piece BF

Club were two of his Irish successes. Woodward believed in allowing free play to the individuality of his artists. He engaged J. Hungerford Pollen to decorate the hammer beam roof of the picture gallery. This artist was also selected by John Henry Newman to decorate his University Church in Stephen's Green. The golden dragons of the gallery roof seem as fresh today as when they were painted more than 100 years ago. They will be preserved in the present restoration. The fine Carrara marble chimneypiece of the gallery was executed by Charles W. Harrison 1834-1903 who was also responsible for the charming monkeys who play around the columns of the Kildare Street Club in Dublin. It is said that the Marchioness of Ormonde arrived daily with flowers and leaves to serve as models for the foliage which covers the entire chimneypiece. The lintel has six panels depicting scenes from the history of the Butler family. It is likely that Harrison also carved the corbels of the gallery and the white marble Moorish-type staircase outside the gallery entrance. This gifted sculptor may have unwittingly contributed to the making of Irish history for it was he who introduced to Ireland the father of Padraig Pearse who was foreman in his establishment in Great Brunswick Street, now Pearse Street, Dublin.

The foundations of a 13th century wall were recently discovered about 12 feet nearer to the river than the present east wing. This may have been part of an extra building running down towards the river which appears on old drawings.

THE SHEE ALMS HOUSE

The Shee Alms House is one of the most interesting buildings in Kilkenny. Founded in 1582 by Sir Richard Shee for the accommodation of twelve poor persons of the City of Kilkenny and endowed under his will, it survived as a charitable institution for three centuries. It is one of the few surviving Tudor Alms Houses in Ireland.

The adjoining Church of St Mary passed to the Church of Ireland at the Reformation and a chapel in the Alms House was used for Catholic worship during the proscribed period. Finance was a problem in the 18th century since the Shees (later Poer-O'Shees) were a Catholic family and were severely hit by the Penal Laws. The lands which supported the Alms House had to be sold and even the Alms House itself passed for a while from their control.

In 1756 one Jasper Rothe, a London merchant and a descendant of a dispossessed Kilkenny family re-endowed the Alms House. His will was proved in Paris where he died and the endowment lasted until the fund was appropriated by the revolutionary French Government in 1789.

Meanwhile the Shee family re-established ownership of the Alms House and administered it jointly with the Catholic Parish of St Mary's. Pensioners were no longer accommodated after about 1830 but it was kept in repair by the Shee Family and used by the Ladies Association of Charity of St Vincent de Paul.

In 1896 it was offered to the Catholic Bishop of Ossory or to any charitable Body which would accept it in the interest of the poor. For reasons which are not clear from contemporary accounts the offer was not accepted.

In 1897 the Kilkenny Archaeological Society also refused an offer of the house for a Museum and Library.

In 1912 it was let as a store. This letting put an end to the long story of the Alms House as a charitable institution. It remains the property of the family who founded it and carries a Preservation Order.

Sir Richard Shee, the founder of the Alms House (d. 1608) was a distinguished lawyer. He belonged to an Irish family of Kerry origin which had migrated to Kilkenny by way of Tipperary.

The Shees became one of the most influential of the ten 'tribes' or civic families of Kilkenny, the only one of Irish origin among them.

Sir Richard was appointed Deputy Treasurer to the Earl of Ormonde (Lord Treasurer of Ireland) in 1576 and was knighted in 1582. During his life-time he acquired a great deal of church property, probably to prevent it falling into the hands of the reformers, and became a very rich man. The founding of the Alms House may have been an attempt to return to the people of Kilkenny some of this wealth since he appears to have been a very religious man.

Three times in his last will he refers to his 'curse' which will descend upon any of his family who alienate or neglect his Alms House. This, perhaps, explains the tenacity with which the family held on to it in the adverse circumstances of the succeeding centuries. There is evidence that the Rothe family were in some way involved in the original foundation through Margaret Rothe, mother of Sir Richard Shee and aunt of John Rothe who built Rothe House. This would explain the legacy of Jasper Rothe in 1756.

Shee Alms House facade **MQ**

Shee Alms House rear **EOD**

The striking Rose Inn Street facade of random rubble contains a doorcase with a drop arch flanked by two two-light Tudor windows with hood mouldings. The first floor contains two small four pane windows and the second floor a two-light window (as on the ground floor) with other miscellaneous openings. The steeply rising ground permits only one floor at the rear. The room behind the rear entrance was used as a Catholic chapel during the eighteenth century. There was then no enclosing wall for St Mary's graveyard and worshippers knelt amongst the tombstones. Worshippers entering the reformed Church of St Mary were tolerant enough to look the other way.

Inscriptions and Escutcheons on Alms House:

Rose Inn Street Facade
Arms of Shee with Latin Inscription translated 'The Arms of Richard Shee Kilkenny Esquire who had this hospital erected in 1582'.

Rear Facade
1 Arms of Shee and Sherlock with Latin inscription translated 'The Arms of Richard Shee Kilkenny Esquire and of Margaret Sherlock, his wife who had this hospital erected 1582'.

2 A Latin passage from Tobias. Translated 'Alms free from death, expiate sin, and open the way to mercy and eternal life'.

ST MARY'S CHURCH & GRAVEYARD

St Mary's Church built at the very beginning of 13th century is but half or less of its original extent. The nave was converted to a Parish Hall in 1960. All the mediaeval monuments, together with the fluted 13th century baptismal font, were removed to the North transept which has a separate entrance. The Garveys, Watons, Archers, Murphys, Dunphys and Rothes are commemorated by fine floriated crosses. The two Renaissance monuments of the Knaresboroughs and Rothes are of black marble and with many quarterings of coats of arms and some original colour. They resemble the Earl of Cork's tomb in St Patrick's Cathedral, Dublin.

In the graveyard is a fine collection of early grave slabs, the effigial one to William Goer and his wife Margareta (c. 1350). The slab to Helen, wife of William of Armoyle is inscribed in Norman-French. Three 16th and early 17th century altar tombs at the East end of the church to the Shee Family are particularly fine, that of Richard Shee (1608) east of the church has a fine superstructure depicting Faith, Hope and Charity. Around the base are shown the 12 Apostles, the only place in Ossory where all 12 are present. One at least of the Shee tombs was made by Walter Kerin and bears his initials.

The tomb of John Rothe FitzPiers the builder of Rothe House is not in its original position. It stands in the graveyard north of the church. Dated 1612 it was erected during the lifetime of John, was the burial place of both himself and his wife Rose Archer and perhaps, also, of Bishop David Rothe who died in 1650. It carries a fine superstructure and is probably the work of Walter Kerin. The Bryan and Shee mausoleums east of the church contain fine 17th century altar tombs.

In a stone screen to the right of the entrance door are six heraldic shields of the old families (Pembrokes, Shees, Rothes, Kellys, Archers, Daniels) which must have been put here for safety many years ago.

They measure roughly 2 ft × 3 ft and are of Kilkenny limestone with a raised surrounding frame and were originally used by the old merchant families to adorn and mark out their homes. No longer in use for their original purpose, they are yet a precious possession of Kilkenny.

Shee mausoleum St Mary's Churchyard   EOD

ROTHE HOUSE

When Rothe House was built by John Rothe in 1594, the Italian Renaissance was at its height and was beginning to influence Irish architecture. Palladio had died fourteen years before; Shakespeare, thirty years old, was writing King Richard III.

Rothe House illustrates how the merchants of Kilkenny lived over their shops and how the streets of the city were lined with arcaded footpaths. The footpath ran within the five round-headed arches the full length of the east frontage and the shop occupied the remainder of the ground floor; the basement, lighted by a series of small windows on the west side, was the store; the living quarters occupied the lofty first floor and the bedrooms were in the roof. Most of the evidence for the arrangement of the living quarters was lost in the nineteenth century, when Timothy O'Hanrahan carried out extensive alterations, but the two original fireplaces and the numerous windows suggest that the first floor was divided into several rooms; the oriel window is modern restoration based upon the tip of the supporting stone corbel which had survived the alterations and the other windows are based upon remains of the original stonework.

A projection at the north-west corner of the building, may have been a stair-turret similar to that at Carrick-on-Suir Castle which, though some twenty years earlier, has many architectural parallels with Rothe House. The house behind the first yard contains much old work, including fireplaces, windows and doorways, but it was greatly altered in the nineteenth century, when the top floor was added.

The second yard is flanked on the north side by outhouses containing seventeenth-century work and on the west side by a much-ruined building of about the same date with remains of a fireplace, windows and other features; on the south side of the yard is the well with a well-head roofed in stone slabs and bearing an inscription dated 1604 mentioning John Rothe and his wife Rose Archer; this same John Rothe, who was the builder of the whole complex of buildings, is recorded by the armorial plaque dated 1594 in the facade centre.

John Rothe FitzPiers and his wife Rose Archer belonged to minor branches of two of the leading civic families of mediaeval Kilkenny. When he died in 1619 business was already being carried on by some of his eleven children and their families.

The house is traditionally associated with the National Ecclesiastical Assembly convened by Bishop Rothe, who was a cousin of John Rothe, in May 1642. This meeting was attended by all the Catholic Bishops of Ireland with representatives of the clergy. It led to the formation of the Parliament of the Confederation in October 1642.

The Rothe family paid dearly for their association with the Confederacy. The house was forfeited in 1653 and the Rothes transplanted to Connaught. An Ormonde connection secured a reprieve in 1660 but the house passed finally from the family in 1691. The survival of the building may be partly due to the fact that it became a school in the 18th century. Among its distinguished pupils were the Banim brothers, in one of whose novels the house is described. A successful branch of the Gaelic League was established and in the early years of the present century Rothe House became a lively centre of Gaelic culture and Nationalist activity, echoing, perhaps, its great days during the Confederation.

The house was bought by Kilkenny Archaeological Society in 1962, restored (under the supervision of Percy Le Clerc) and opened as a museum and library in 1966.

Courtyards, Rothe House O

14th century Jug, Rothe House Museum NM

Rothe House facade MQ

East window, St Francis' Abbey   GD

Support figure, St Francis' Abbey   CPW

Support figure, St Francis' Abbey   CPW

ST FRANCIS ABBEY

This abbey (more correctly friary) of the Franciscans was founded between 1231 and 1234 by Richard Marshall, Third Earl of Pembroke. In 1331 Dame Isabella Palmer extended the Chancel and erected the high altar and present east window, which extends almost the entire height and width of the church and consists of a seven-light window.

In 1347 a confraternity was established to raise funds for a bell tower, but in the following year the Black Death devastated the country and was chronicled by one of the friars, John Clyn. It was probably not completed until much later in the century. The six tiny sculptured figures supporting the bearing shafts of the groining of the tower are most unusual. Instead of the conventional head of a monk or angel we have six lay figures exhibiting various expressions of the pain and stress involved in literally supporting the structure. One, a female figure has money in her hand so that these are taken to represent the benefactors who shouldered the responsibility of financing the building of the tower in that bleak era following the decimation by the Black Death.

In 1540 the friary was suppressed and its properties granted to the Corporation. The subsequent ruin of the monastery was accelerated by the seemingly inevitable building of a barracks in the grounds (see also St John's Priory). Only the chancel and bell tower of the church were spared together with the sacristy, recently restored as the oratory of Smithwicks Brewery.

There are numerous records of burials which took place in the monastery graveyard but its whereabouts are no longer known. Any further demolitions in the area of Barrack Lane should be carefully carried out, as monuments may still come to light.

Excavations carried out some years ago established the presence of a large transept and aisle on the north side in which some graves were found. The cloister was to the south and is now covered with buildings. The Friars Well, with its stone circular superstructure close to the Nore was also extant until a few years ago.

13th century tombstone found 1977 TB

The Black Abbey BA

THE BLACK ABBEY

The Black Abbey or the Convent of the One and Undivided Trinity was founded by William Marshall the younger, Earl of Pembroke, for the Dominican Friars in 1225. The site was an unfortunate one as subsequent events proved, for to this day, it is subjected almost annually to severe flooding. Despite this handicap the Abbey has shown vitality and tenacity of life rare in monastic institutions. From its earliest days it occupied a place of importance in the civic life of the community. The 'Great Twelve', the governing body of the early Norman town, frequently met there, as we are told in the Liber Primus; and the Lords Justices stayed there when they came to carry out their legal functions.

The Abbey was dissolved in 1543 and was granted to the Sovereign and Burgesses of Kilkenny. It was converted for use as a Courthouse but the people moved in and built their houses in the shelter of its walls. An old print shows us these thatched hovels clinging like limpets to the ancient walls. At the end of the 18th century it ceased to be used as a Courthouse and became for a time a roofless ruin. The Friars, however had remained in the neighbourhood and one of them — Father Vincent Meade — secured a lease of the ruins from the Tynte Family of County Wicklow and succeeded in roofing and restoring a portion of the Abbey in 1778; not however until well into the 19th century was it fully opened for public worship.

The present building includes the restored nave and ancient tower house, which serves as an organ gallery, together with the large early fourteenth century south transept and magnificent window with its fine intersected tracery. The high, square bell tower with its attractive Irish-style stepped battlements was built around 1505. An inscribed stone at the base requests prayers for the soul of 'James Shortall, Lord of Ballylarkin and Ballykeefe and his wife Katherine White' who gave the workmen employed in the erection of this tower their daily pay from beginning to end. The bell which had been removed to Dunlavin, Co Wicklow, after the supression was restored in 1925.

An unusual sculpture in alabaster of the Blessed Trinity may be seen near the high altar. This was found hidden in a wall of the ruin during the 19th century restoration and bears the inscription, in arabic numerals, 1264.

At the entrance, a line of monuments on the left consists of eleven slabs (some of which may have been coffin lids), four stone coffins and a water trough. These were found within the precincts of the Abbey at different times from 1816 onwards. Some, apparently, within the church, some in the destroyed chancel and some in the cloister area adjoining Friars Bridge Street. The stone coffins are thought to belong to the 13th century. There is also an effigy of a lady which can be dated by her dress to the 16th century.

In a niche in the transept is a small oaken mutilated figure of St Dominic — the only statue of St Dominic known to survive in Ireland.

In the Priory building is a 14th century stone figure of St Catherine of Alexandria (said to have been found in a wall cavity in 1825), a wooden Madonna and child of the 16th century, and one of the earliest printed books — printed in Paris in 1475. A confederate banner once in the possession of the Black Abbey is now in the Dominican Priory of Tallaght. The Abbey is now undergoing restoration.

ST CANICE'S CATHEDRAL

The thirteenth century Cathedral of St Canice stands overlooking the northern end of the city. Surrounding it are the remnants of its close, comprising the Bishop's Palace, the Deanery, St Canice's Library and several of the prebendal residences.

The present building was preceded by an early monastic settlement, and subsequently a small Hiberno-Romanesque Church, which in turn was replaced by the present Cathedral. The round tower (31m high) alone survives from the Monastery (it then had a conical cap) when it was used as a belfry and a refuge in times of danger.

The Cathedral was begun by Hugh de Rous (1202-1218) in the Early Gothic style from the Angevin district in France, continued by his successors, and completed during the episcopacy of Geoffrey St. Leger (1260-1286). Despite an eventful history, including the iconoclasm of the Reformation in the mid-sixteenth century, wrecking by the Cromwellians in the mid-seventeenth century and restoration in the mid-eighteenth century, the Cathedral is unusually consistent in style. Its present appearance is due to a general restoration begun in 1866 by the Architect Sir Thomas Newenham Deane.

The building — Ireland's second largest mediaeval Cathedral — is symmetrical in plan: a cruciform church with aisled nave of 5 bays, choir cum chancel flanked on either side by two chapels of the same size projecting from the transepts, a low central tower (a lofty central bell tower collapsed in 1332) and a porch. Although large, it was not a particularly ambitious church, and the unadorned architecture gives a wonderful sense of light and space.

The oldest part of the building is the chancel which was possibly completed prior to 1220, and contains a fine three light east window. This window once contained celebrated early mid-fourteenth century stained glass, which having survived the Reformation, was subject to a purchase bid by Rinucinni (the Papal Nuncio at the Confederation of Kilkenny) in 1645. The offer was refused and in 1651 the glass was smashed by Cromwell's troops. The transepts were probably built around 1250 while the nave has features which have been dated to around 1260. The absence of a stone vaulted roof permits widely spaced piers, the bases and capitals of which have robust horizontal mouldings. The quatrefoil sectional shape of these piers is echoed in the clerestorey windows and the spandrel in the west doorway. This doorway is the finest surviving early Gothic doorway in Ireland and features many foliage cusps and two fine label-stops in the form of a human head.

The master-mason for much of this late work is known as the Gowran Master since his handiwork is most noticeable at Gowran church — some of his characteristics appear at Thomastown. As a sculptor he was perhaps the most gifted craftsman in Ireland during the thirteenth century.

The tower had fallen in 1332 and was restored by Bishop Hackett (1460-1478) and the beautiful fan-vaulting perforated for bell ropes dates from this period.

The interior contains some interesting architectural features. In the south nave aisle is a thirteenth century font, which, with its fluted sides is peculiar to the Diocese of Ossory. Beneath the central light of the west window is a unique gallery with trefoil arches approached by a staircase in the thickness of the wall. A very unusual aumbry in the chapel of the north transept, instead of being arched, is rect-

Piers and Margaret tomb PDI

St Canice's Cathedral BF

angularly stepped, terminating in a square head.

St Kieran's Chair in the north transept is used for the ceremonial enthronement of Bishops. Beneath it is a great stone which tradition asserts was transferred with the See of Ossory from Aghaboe and earlier from the first settlement of St Kieran at Sier-Kieran.

North nave aisle: several monuments by the O'Tunney Family, e.g. an armoured effigy in high relief, a side slab with Apostles.

North transept: canopied tomb of which the three west figures (probably from another tomb) are probably by Rory O'Tunney.

South choir aisle: Bishop David Rothe Memorial erected originally in the Lady Chapel when the Catholics recovered the Cathedral in 1642.

South transept: Piers, 8th Earl of Ormond (d. 1539) and Margaret Fitzgerald (d. 1542), his countess — effigies in high relief. James, 9th Earl of Ormond (d. 1546) — armoured effigy.

South nave aisle: Richard Butler, 1st Viscount Mountgarret (d. 1571), effigy in 'white armour'. Honoria Shortall (nee Grace, d. 1596), the front panel of the tomb is from another monument (possibly by Rory O'Tunney).

Besides the finest collection of sixteenth century monuments in Ireland (many of which were smashed in 1651 and incorrectly assembled subsequently) there is a fine collection of early seventeenth century floorslabs to tradesmen, including a shoemaker, a weaver and a carpenter, showing the emblems of their trade. There are two interesting stained glass windows in the south wall of the nave. The Loftus Memorial window is dated 1931 and is by A. E.

The West Door MF

14th century tomb detail AP

Library window EOD

Child and the Connellan window at the western end is by Sarah Purser and Ethel M. Rhind and was executed about 1918.

Sarah Purser was co-founder with Edward Martyn of An Tur Gloinne in 1903 and A. E. Child was the first artist to teach there. The movement achieved great success and inspired such stained-glass artists as Harry Clarke, Michael Healy and Evie Hone.

The only other windows in the city from this school are the three fine windows (5 lights) in St Kieran's College (c. 1935) by C. B. Simmonds of the Harry Clarke Studios.

The Whyte Memorial Window (1934) in St Patrick's Catholic Church is a product of the Earley Studios of Camden Street, Dublin and is influenced by the Harry Clarke technique.

ST CANICE'S LIBRARY

The site of St Canice's Library and some, at least, of the present structure date back to the 13th century, when as Manse House of the Prebendary of Blackrath, it formed part of the ancient Irishtown wall. The lower walls of the west and north of the existing house are part of this defensive rampart.

The house had fallen into disrepair by the time of the foundation of the Earl of Ormonde's School, sited here (1539). Richard Stanihurst, the historian, was the most distinguished pupil of that School, as Peter White, Fellow of Oriel College, Oxford, was its most renowned Schoolmaster. In 1565, Peter White was made Dean of Waterford. On his departure the School went into an irreversible decline. Captain John Joener, an officer in the Cromwellian Army, took away the main timber of the schoolhouse for use in building a house 'within a mile of Kilkenny commonly called Joener's Folly' — a label which is still affixed to the townland in question.

Bishop Thomas Otway, who died in 1693 bequeathed his books and £200 in money, 'and more if needful', for the beginning of a library for the use of the clergy about the Cathedral Church of St Canice. It was sited in the upper storey of the old Schoolhouse.

The establishment of St Canice's Library makes it the earliest Diocesan Library in Ireland.

Otway's legacy was augmented in 1756 when Bishop Edward Maurice bequeathed his library of books and ten cases of Danzig oak to the library. These books form the major portion of the present collection, and seven of the ten presses are still in the library room.

Bishop Maurice also ordered that the books be catalogued, but it was not until 1895 that a full catalogue was compiled by the Librarian, Rev George Warburton Rooke. This catalogue is lodged in the Library of the Representative Body of the Church of Ireland in Dublin.

When Dr McAdoo became Bishop in 1962, he initiated a scheme of purchasing a limited number of books each year. Thus the Library established nigh on three hundred years ago, continues as a service for the clergy and laity of the United Dioceses of Ossory, Ferns and Leighlin.

The Palace GT

The Robing Room GD

THE BISHOP'S PALACE

No written account of this unusual house exists but its story can be deduced in part from the building itself and from certain historical facts known about it. These latter are scanty enough but, taken together with aspects of the construction of the house, they throw light on the building and help to account for some of its intriguing architectural features.

Some time after 1354 Bishop Ledrede, Alice Kyteler's antagonist, obtained royal permission to take down the three churches of St Nicholas, St Brigid and St James. The bishop used the material to build a house near the Cathedral and he perpetuated the dedications by erecting therein an altar to the three saints. The present chapel bears the same dedications.

An examination of the house indicates that the earliest part consists of what was obviously a fourteenth-century keep at the eastern end of the house. The ground floor of the keep has a groined ceiling supported by a central pillar. During renovations in 1962/63 a stone staircase was discovered in the east wall of the first floor and a slit window was also revealed in the north wall. This section of the house is almost certainly Ledrede's original building.

What is not equally clear is the relationship of the entrance hall and chapel (which constitute the front portion of the ground floor of the present house) to the original keep. These rooms have, like the keep, groined ceilings which are carried on stone pillars. Whether this section was contemporary with the keep or added later is not known. The suggestion has been made that this part of the house may have been built by Bishop Griffith Williams (1641-1672), but this seems most unlikely as the structure suggests an earlier period, (possibly fifty years later than the keep). It is known, however, that Williams carried out extensive repairs in 1661, when he returned from exile, having been driven out by Cromwell in company with most of the bishops of the Church of Ireland. Contemporary records show that he found the house and the Cathedral in a ruinous state on his return. His work of renovation is commemorated by the altar which was made for the present Chapel in 1962, exactly three centuries later.

In the garden stands a little building, still known locally as the 'Robing Room' or 'The Colonnade'. The 'Colonnade' obviously refers to the Doric colonnade which formerly ran from it to the north transept door of the Cathedral (the dividing road between the garden and the churchyard did not then exist). It was built by Bishop Pococke, probably about the time of his restoration of the Cathedral in 1756.

The house appears to have been improved by Bishop John Parry (1672-1677) and again by Bishop Charles Este (1735-1741). By the year 1739, as can be seen from an engraving of that date, the house had assumed its present shape, save that the third floor was an attic storey with dormer windows set in a sloping roof.

It can also be seen that the drawing-room and dining-room (a two storey addition fitted into the angle of what had by then become an L-shaped house) were in existence at that date. These are typically elegant Georgian rooms, having curved ends and doors, and, in the case of the dining-room, two handsome wooden pillars. The entrance hall, and very fine staircase, with its carved ornamentation, has a seventeenth-century feel in its design, particularly in the shape of the windows, though some of the moulding must clearly date from the eighteenth century.

The house is therefore an amalgam of houses and styles and its appearance externally is completely deceptive, since at some time after 1739, the attic storey was altered by the facade of the house being raised and the roof-pitch lowered to give a Georgian appearance to the whole.

It seems fair, therefore, to claim it as being among the oldest inhabited houses in Leinster and it contains portraits and other reminders of many of its past occupants. The list includes such names as Nicholas Walsh, the first to introduce printing in Irish type in the sixteenth century, and who had the services printed in Irish and commenced an Irish translation of the New Testament; Richard Pococke, the famous eighteenth-century traveller and antiquary, a benefactor of Kilkenny; Hugh Hamilton, the learned mathematician who was one of the founders of the Royal Irish Academy, and Charles Dodgson, grandfather of the author of Alice in Wonderland.

THE PRIORY OF ST JOHN THE EVANGELIST

Founded early in the 13th century by William Marshall the elder, Earl of Pembroke, for the Canons Regular of St Augustine to replace an earlier house situated at 'the head of the Bridge of Kilkenny', a site which was obviously considered unsuitable. The Canons had already been endowed with the tithes of all the provisions of the Castle of Kilkenny and they continued to receive many rich endowments from time to time. When in 1540 the Priory was suppressed by Henry VIII, Richard Cantwell, the last Prior, surrendered an extensive list of possessions belonging to the Priory. In 1645 the Catholics were again in possession and a grant was made to the Jesuits for a college or seminary. They were however driven out by Cromwell in 1650 but remained in the town where they established an oratory. In 1690 under James II they applied to the Corporation to be restored but in the meantime the Capuchins had taken over a plot of ground in the Priory grounds and had so improved it ('the meanest and craggiest spot in this city') that the Corporation were unwilling to disturb them. In a few years the Catholic Corporation was swept away and Jesuits and Capuchins banished.

Of the Priory nothing now remains but the Lady Chapel (c. 1290), which was re-roofed in 1817 as a Protestant parish church, and the ruined chancel of the Conventual church. The nave still stood until 1780 when it was demolished and the material used to build an infantry barracks (now the Evans Asylum).

Such was the number of windows in the Lady Chapel that it was known as the Lantern of Ireland — the surviving east window dates to around 1300.

The roofless chancel marred by a lean-to building, contains a beautiful six-light

Chancel, St John's Priory   EOD

east window of c. 1250. A notable tomb is the Purcell monument in the N.E. end of the Chancel which contains an effigy in high relief of a Purcell knight with his lady in a long flowing robe and horned head-dress. The head and feet of the male figure are broken off. An inscription is dated 1500.

The Priory was a walled monastery and must have been extensive since all the land of Michael Street belonged to it. Carved stones are still to be found in the gardens of these houses — two recent finds indicate there were more effigial tombs and a finely carved cloister. The only out-building left is the fragmentary remains of a small church or oratory about 100 yards to the west of the main church. This building was rib-vaulted with two of the remaining capitals ornamented with human cowled heads and fine dog-toothing respectively. It may have been attached to the Prior's residence since the land between it and the river is known as Prior's Orchard. Beside the Priory is a square 3 storey building which is probably a rebuilt monastic structure.

For Evan's Poor House which occupies part of the monastery grounds, see page 95.

2

*The Character
of Kilkenny*

St Canice's Steps O

Kenny's Well GD

The overall character of Kilkenny derives not only from its monuments and its individual buildings of great character.

Much of its character derives from its narrow streets, laneways, steps and square which to no small extent are a consequence of the development of the City within the confines of the City Wall.

During Tudor times, a number of families, including the Archers, Shees, Langtons and Rothes, prospered and left their marks on the City which survive to this day.

For many centuries Kilkenny has fostered a tradition of education and literature which undoubtedly has played its part in the formation of the City's character. Outsiders not only associate Kilkenny with its architectural heritage and its history, but with its cultural tradition. A tradition which is being maintained today with the presence of young craftsmen (many of whom are attracted to the area by the sympathetic character of the town), the initiating of the Kilkenny Arts Week, etc.

KENNY'S WELL

This clear spring on the south bank of the little Bregagh river in Kennyswell Street, a quarter mile south west of St Canice's Cathedral, may well be the earliest settlement of the town of Kilkenny.

Nothing but its name and a strong oral tradition associates it with the Saint. Yet it was in such valleys that the hermit saints often began their missions which grew, in time, into Celtic monasteries.

The treachery of this tortuous low-lying stream today with its propensity for sudden flooding would readily explain why the first wooden church of St Canice was built on the nearby eminence to be followed in due course by its protective round tower which stands today next to the Cathedral.

Just as the well retains its reverence as a place of pilgrimage and supplication, so too does the quaint old stone structure which covers it, retain the outline of an early celtic church though it was probably built in the 18th century. Who knows what structure preceded it.

Needless to say, the well and its field belonged to the See of Ossory from the foundation of that See in Kilkenny. Some time between 1224 and 1250 Bishop Geoffrey de Turville granted to the Dominicans of the Black Abbey permission to draw water from it on condition that the circumference of the conduit would be no bigger than the episcopal ring, and to make certain of this a facsimile ring was attached to the Charter.

The well, still in the hands of the Dominicans, once was surmounted by a small cross, broken by vandals around 1935.

TALBOT'S CASTLE AND CITY WALL

The Mediaeval town of Kilkenny was well fortified by stong walls and bastions of which there are some remains extant. The map executed by John Rocque in 1758 shows the outline of the main wall which surrounded the Norman town founded by William Marshall. The Irishtown to the North was also fortified but these walls were not so formidable and very few traces remain. From historians and the municipal archives we have information as to how the walls and bastions were maintained and how the gates were manned and 'the Watch' organised. In times of turbulence particularly after the Battle of the Boyne extra precautions were taken. The black circles appearing at intervals along on the map indicate where bastions were sited.

The first of these on the south side is still extant. A strongly built massive circular tower, it stands in the courtyard of the City Technical School and is known as Talbot's Castle. From that point the Wall turned at right angles and ran along at the rear of the Patrick Street houses forming the boundary wall of their gardens. In the garden of the Provincial Bank may be seen a small bastion and evidence of a 'sallyport' or small wall opening. The best example of the wall still surviving and most easily accessible runs from the top of Collier's Lane to James Street and forms the boundary wall of the Presentation Convent grounds. The outline of the original defence loopholes may be seen. Unfortunately a portion of it is rapidly becoming enveloped in ivy. The

Black Freren Gate MF

remaining bastions and the gateways all of which had houses or 'castles' built over them have been removed from time to time to make way for new buildings or wider roadways. Only an arch of one gateway now remains in Abbey Street. A lease of the upper rooms of the Castle over this gate was made in October 1633 by Stephen Daniel. He undertook to build the said Castle and 'cover same with oaken timber and slate staunch and tenantable'. The gate was known as the Black Freren Gate; a portion of the old wall or possibly a later reconstruction of it is adjoining.

From here the wall ran to the river Bregagh and followed the line of the river to the Nore. Where it enters the Nore in the grounds of the Franciscan Monastery, now part of the premises of Messrs Smithwick's Brewery, there is a small bastion known as Evans Turret. The land on which it stands was part of the grounds of the Franciscan Monastery which had been leased by the Corporation to Alderman Evans in 1724 and remained with his descendants for over a century.

Market Slip GD

THE SLIPS

Notable features of Kilkenny are the narrow lanes which run through the city. The stepped lanes running from High Street to Kieran Street and from St Mary's to Rose Inn Street are locally known as The Slips.

The Slip at Rose Inn Street runs between Mr Brennan's butchers Stall, No 25, and No 24, Mr Parson's shop, once The Bush Inn.

Near the City Hall is the Butter Slip which runs between Nos 79 and 80, High Street. The site of this slip was part of the local Abbey property vested in the Corporation at the time of the suppression of the monasteries. In 1602 Nicholas Langton obtained a Fee Farm grant of the premises from the Municipal Body, binding himself to leave open through it a public passage communicating between High Street and what was then called 'Low Lane'. The passage exists to the present day under the designation of the Butter Slip. It conforms exactly to the measurements laid down in the

Rocque's Map of Kilkenny 1758 NL

Agreement. Though not now suitable, as was intended, for horses and carriages, it is used by foot passengers and steps have been provided to facilitate them. In an alcove in the north wall, a woman sold butter giving the name to the slip. The High Street end was renovated by An Taisce in 1970.

Further north in High Street we find another stepped slip leading down to the Market Yard. Open stalls were set up by the butchers in this slip to sell tripe and veal to people going down to the market. Sad to relate, the old cobble stones and flags were removed from these slips some years ago and replaced by cement.

Perhaps the most charming of all the stepped passageways are the two which rise from St Kieran's Street to St Mary's Church, one quite near the Butter Slip and the other at the Rose Inn Street end of St Kieran's Street.

They are very narrow and steep with a bend which invites the traveller to investigate further. Before the graveyard was walled they led straight to the Church. Now they skirt the walls and find egress to High Street through a small door at the back of the Tholsel forecourt.

A Tudor Chimney, Patrick St EOD

TUDOR KILKENNY

A period of stability and prosperity occurred in Kilkenny from about 1580 to 1640. It resulted in the building by the merchants and land-owners of elaborate stone houses and of splendid sculptured tombs. Many of the latter remain in St Canice's, St Mary's and St John's and fragments of the former are still to be found in the city.

Rothe House and the Shee Alms House survived intact and the row of escutcheons at the entrance to St Mary's Church were probably retrieved from those houses which were destroyed. In some cases the escutcheons were left on the facades of the houses and so these can be identified with the families who built them.

Archer

Numbers 17, 18 and 19 High Street all formed the family house of the Archers. The armorial bearings are those of Martin Archer and the house is dated 1582. Its octagonal stone chimney was removed for

The Hole in the Wall COC

safety to Rothe House some years ago. At the rear its early foundation is still visible. Narrow passages, gothic doorways and Tudor fragments are to be seen everywhere. It followed the pattern of Rothe House and included several houses divided by courtyards. In the eighteenth century the most westerly of its houses became the famous 'Hole in the Wall'. This was the great supper-house of Kilkenny for about 100 years (1750-1850). The tavern was patronised by the young blades of the day and numbered among its patrons John, 17th Earl of Ormonde (known as Jack of the Castle), Henry Grattan, Henry Flood, Sir Hercules Langrishe, Sir Jonah Barrington and the Duke of Wellington. Popular tradition describes it thus:

'If ever you go to Kilkenny
Remember the Hole in the Wall
You may there get blind drunk for a penny
Or tipsy for nothing at all'.

Later owners of the Archer House were the Shearman family, printers, one of whom was the historian and archaeologist Father John Francis Shearman. Thomas Mac Donagh and Francis Sheehy-Skeffington lived here from about 1901 to 1903, when they were teaching in St Kieran's College.

Shee

This family had many houses in Kilkenny. Numbers 98 and 99 High Street (Woolworths) survived intact until the nineteen twenties when all its Tudor features with the exception of the escutcheon were removed in spite of spirited protests voiced by Kilkenny citizens. The arms are those of Henry Shee and Frances Crisp his wife.

The Shee House which was used for the Confederate Parliament was taken down about 100 years ago. A plaque at the entrance to the Market car park in Parliament Street marks its site.

The House of Elias Shee, ancestor of the Archer-Shee family is 68 High Street. It still retains a splendid mantel-piece adorned by the Shee arms. The house extends to St Kieran's Street where the escutcheon on this facade is intact. A descendant of this family was the cadet George Archer Shee whose dramatic acquittal on a charge of stealing a 5/- postal order inspired the successful play 'The Winslow Boy'. The boy, a Catholic, was defended by Sir Edward Carson. Another descendant was the famous portrait painter Sir Martin Archer Shee.

Langton

Nicholas Langton, one of Kilkenny's first Aldermen built a great stone house in 1609. It occupied both sides of the Butter Slip and extended from High Street to Kieran's Street. The Langtons lived here for nearly 200 years. Since Nicholas had 25 children, it is not surprising that he acquired a second house at Danville on the Bennetsbridge Road. The Langton name is still common in Kilkenny. The plan of the house was somewhat similar to Rothe House and traces of the street arcading remain as well as Tudor windows at the rear. The escutcheon which disappeared in quite recent times bore the arms of Nicholas Langton and Lettice Daniel, his wife.

Rothe

The house of Edward Rothe (Carrigan's shop next to the Tholsel) also retained some 16th century features in the rear. A chimney piece was removed to Rothe House for safety in 1963. Edward Rothe was a nephew of Bishop David Rothe and it is thought that the latter may have died here during the Cromwellian conquest of Kilkenny.

Other family houses identified by their escutcheons are FitzGerald-Shee (Desmond branch of FitzGerald) in No 79 (Rush) John Street; an Archer house in Nos 1, 2 and 3 (V.G. Supermarket) Parliament Street of which the escutcheon is in private hands (Archer and Shee arms); and an Archdeacon house in Dean Street (site now a blank wall on the southern side). The arms are those of Archdeacon and Woodlock and the escutcheon is preserved in Rothe House. The beautiful Georgian house adjoining John's Bridge has many Tudor features at the rear. It is not known what family built it originally, but it may have been the Ormonde Butlers since Charles Butler, Earl of Arran and brother to the 2nd Duke of Ormonde was in possession in 1704 and it was almost certainly the Butlers who rebuilt it at the end of that century.

Doorcase, Kieran's St MF

GEORGIAN KILKENNY

It is scarcely possible to extricate Georgian Kilkenny from Tudor Kilkenny. A Georgian structure may be built upon a Tudor basement or a classical facade give way to a Tudor rear.

The Parade, opposite the Castle, has the greatest length of Georgian terrace ending in the splendid Castle Stables, now the Design Workshops. This lovely terrace should be viewed from the formal garden of the Castle through the lime trees to appreciate its beauty.

Patrick Street includes Butler House with a magnificent interior. It was remodelled about 1780 by adding two bays at the back. This street also has the Club House Hotel, which began as a fox-hunting club in the late 18th century and whose interior has remained substantially intact. Some Georgian houses on the opposite side have unusual Tudor chimneys and basement features.

Doorcase, 3 John's Quay EOD

Doorcase, Kilkenny College EOD

The High Street is dominated by the Tholsel or City Hall (1761). It replaced an earlier Tholsel of 1575, slightly further back from the street. Possibly the existence of its predecessor accounts for the appearance of the present building which in some ways seems pre-Georgian, consisting of a double arcade five arches in length. Overhead is the great Council chamber running the whole length of the building. The steeply pitched roof is crowned by a balcony and a graceful clock tower. The architect is unknown but popular tradition credits it to an Italian. It certainly resembles buildings in cities such as Florence used for the same purpose — the display of saleable goods. Such commerce was carried on in the arcaded portion of the Tholsel until early in the present century.

Parliament Street has the earliest buildings. Nos 42 and 43 were built very early in the 18th century and are now part of a terrace which includes later houses. Though built independently, a common theme of simple plasterwork and cornice moulding runs through them all.

St Kieran's Street has an impressive pair of Georgian houses, Nos 12 and 13. The doorcases of cut limestone are narrow but well proportioned with finely executed detail. Houses such as these will never rank as great architecture but they lend charm to a provincial town.

A number of similar houses are to be seen in William Street, Chapel Lane and Wellington Square. In the latter two, an unusual feature is the inclusion of the two doors, each with separate fan-light in one round headed door recess two feet in depth.

Just beside St John's Bridge is a Tudor house which belonged to the Ormonde Butlers and was remodelled by them in the 18th century. The interior has some very beautiful plaster work which may now be in danger from its age. See page 97, John Street.

Kilkenny College (1782) is a fine square building in a pleasent situation on the river bank. It has a splendid doorcase and fanlight. Farther up the river on the west bank is an 18th century 'Tea house' or garden pavilion. This is a most unusual little building to appear in a provincial town. It was re-roofed in 1976 when its chimney stack was removed.

Another small gem of the 18th century worthy of restoration is the robing room in the Palace grounds opposite the north door of the Cathedral of St Canice. It was built by Bishop Pococke about 1756.

St James Asylum, south of the Castle, though built in 1803 is entirely classical with a lovely gateway facing the tree lined road to the Castle gate. James Switzir, a contractor, who made a considerable profit from the contract to build the military barracks, decided to present the town with an almshouse, which he built himself. In a niche in the end wall appears the founder looking gloriously pompous and not at all like a provincial building contractor. He is reading from a book which is inscribed with the words 'I am thankful to Thee, O my God for this and all Thy blessings through Thy dear Son Jesus Christ Amen'. Can it be that chief among those blessings he numbered the delight of living in 18th century Kilkenny? See page 49, Castle Road.

18th century tea-house EOD

KILKENNY WRITERS

Kilkenny as a town has always accorded a considerable measure of respect to education and literature. The tradition has persisted since in 1539 Piers, 8th Earl of Ormonde and his Countess founded a school in St Canice's Churchyard which was to achieve fame for its master and its pupils in contemporary records.

David Rothe, Bishop of Ossory (1618-1650), Theologian, historian and a writer of the greatest literary distinction was a brilliant star in the 17th century firmament.

In the next century such notable literary figures as Swift, Congreve, and Berkeley received their education here.

The 19th century produced the Banim brothers, novelists. They set themselves the task of changing the currently accepted picture of the Irish peasant as a comic figure and drunken buffoon. In a series of novels called 'Tales by the O'Hara Family' they revealed the appalling conditions under which the Irish peasant lived and undoubtedly succeeded in arousing sympathy and a better understanding of the Irish character in England.

Later in the century the journals of the Kilkenny Archaeological Society and the Ossory Archaeological Society provided an opportunity for native historians to record their investigations into the history of the city and county.

In the early years of the present century, a talented family of writers emerged — the Hacketts of Patrick Street, while from 19 Michael Street came another brilliant novelist Francis McManus also known for his work as Features Editor for RTE.

The following are the principal works of some of the Kilkenny writers:

John Banim by E Fitzpatrick

Francis McManus by Sean O'Sullivan

John Banim (1798-1842)
Poet, playwright and novelist. He is best known for the series of novels entitled 'Tales by the O'Hara Family' written in conjunction with his brother Michael. The series included The Boyne Water (reprinted by University of Lille in 1976), Crohoore of The Billhook, The Nowlans, The Croppy, The Last Baron of Crana and The Conformists. His last work was Father Connell.

Michael Banim (1796-1864)
Besides collaborating with his brother on 'Tales by the O'Hara Family', his own novels were Clough Finn (1852) and The Town of the Cascades (1864).

Francis Hackett (1883-1962)
His best known work is Henry VIII (1929). He also wrote The Green Lion (1935) based on his childhood in Kilkenny, Francis I (1934), Queen Anne Boleyn (1939), The Senator's Last Night, a novel (1943) and an early novel That Nice Young Couple. He died in Denmark where he had lived with his Danish wife, playwright Signe Toksvig.

Florence Hackett (1884-1963)
Sister of Francis Hackett wrote a novel 'With Benefit of Clergy' published in New York in 1923 and many plays and short stories. Her plays have been produced on Radio Eireann and most of her stories appeared in the Dublin Magazine.

Francis McManus (1909-1965)
Wrote travel books, short stories, essays, biographies and history. His novels include Stand and Give Challenge (1935), Candle for the Proud (1936), Men Withering (1939), The Wild Garden (1940), Flow on Lovely River (1941), Watergate (1942), The Greatest of These (1943), Statue for a Square (1945), The Fire in the Dust (1951), and American Son (1959). He was appointed Director of Talks and Features in Radio Eireann in 1947. A feature of some of his novels is the authentic picture he draws of life in Kilkenny in the nineteen-twenties.

3
*The Streets
of Kilkenny*

The Parade EOD

From very early in its history until about 1930, Kilkenny's streets were paved with the local grey unpolished marble. It has often been called 'The Marble City'. These hard flags had the capacity for throwing off the water before it turned to mud. A few of them could still be preserved at Velvet Lane.

For many centuries, also, the houses were heated with the smokeless Castlecomer anthracite coal which causes little air pollution. An old jingle thus describes the city:

'Fire, without smoke
Air without fog
Water without mud
Land without bog'.

No-one knows its author, but it was already old when recited to John Dunton, a visitor of 1680.

The future of most of the buildings described on previous pages is assured. However, the overall character of Kilkenny derives not so much from its monuments and its individual buildings of great architectural character as from lesser buildings and groups of buildings, buildings closing the view down a street, the effect of sunlight highlighting the texture of a wall or dancing on the panes of a window, and fine shopfronts — some with signwriting of great beauty. Many of these elements are in themselves often quite commonplace and hence liable to be swept away or altered without regard. It is the summation of these elements which give a scale and character to the town which has been lost or destroyed in many other towns in the Country, and which could all too easily be sacrificed in Kilkenny if great care is not taken to conserve it.

Not only is the visual summation of these elements important but also the uses to which these elements are put. The character of a town centre is considerably affected by the inhabitants who put life into the buildings. It is thus necessary to retain the existing balance between the residential and commercial use of buildings — a balance which can only be maintained if due regard is given to the problems created by traffic and the provision of amenities.

Section 3 is an inventory of many of the City Centre buildings and indicates features of interest which the observer may not notice because that feature may be thought commonplace or, if it is a matter of historical fact, be hidden.

Once aware of such features, the observer may come to cherish the building in which he lives. If he is a person responsible for the well-being of the City, he may recognise the value of its architecture to the community. If a visitor, he may pass more pleasurably from one major building to another and be more appreciative of the diversity of the town and its wealth of architectural detail. All will more readily be able to decide what they do, or do not want in this town, or their hometown.

In Section 3 of this book code letters have been used in the headings to convey the following classification of buildings:

A   Outstanding architectural quality
B   High architectural quality
C   Quality as a period example
H   Historical association and value
S   Scenic value as part of city's character

The Bank of Ireland by M Lunt

THE PARADE

This splendid street almost as wide as it is long runs up-hill from the central crossroads of the city to the Castle Gate. Tree-lined and bordered by a secluded walk, here citizens may sit and contemplate the hustle and bustle of a lively town. Here the old soldier of the Confederate wars, James Butler, 1st Duke of Ormonde, held his military parades and trained his grandson in the art of war. Hence the name which has survived for 300 years.

The scene of many exciting public meetings in the great days of open-air politics, this fine open space should be kept as clear as possible of kerbstones, traffic signs and other obstructions.

West Side: Nos 1 — 3   C

Bank of Ireland, built in 1870. Two fine buildings, namely the Bank and the Imperial Hotel, dominate the northern end of the Parade. This impressive stone bank was erected in 1870 to the design of Sandham Symes of Dublin. The main entrance porch features two rusticated columns; panels of rustication occur beneath some of the ground floor windows and some of the quoins are rusticated. The first floor windows have pedimented aedicules but the whole building is marred by modern signs cutting the windows in two.

No 4   S

This building replaced the old Kilkenny Private Theatre where plays had been staged in the early nineteenth century and which brought fame and visitors from all parts of England and Ireland. The present building was erected in 1853 as the Atheneum Assembly Rooms and used for general community purposes for the remainder of the century. It is now occupied by the Revenue Commissioners.

Nos 7 — 10   B

This attractive four storey Georgian Terrace was built around 1791, and although Nos 8 and 9 have been plastered the group retains a unified dignity through the use of an appropriate colour.

No 7: A 3 storey building with a brick facade over a basement and fronted by railings which contain a boot-scraper. The windows on the second floor have sashes of 3 and 6 panes; on the other floors 6 pane sashes. The stone surround to the fanlighted door atop a flight of steps has a pair of engaged Tuscan columns. The original roof has been replaced.

Nos 8 and 9: Although the facades of the terrace are similar the railings in front of each house differ and here straight railings flank six steps to two adjacent fanlighted doors.

No. 10: A brick 5 bay facade, the largest in the terrace. From 1835 to around 1871 the Bank of Ireland occupied this building. Steps and curved railings (with boot-scraper) lead up to a fine stone door surround with a delicately carved lintel, flanked by a patera, and on a pair of engaged Tuscan columns.

No 11   C

A. G. Davis. A 3 storey 5 bay pebbledashed facade. The limestone Gibbsian door surround has a fluted lintel. The 3-centre arched coach entrance is attractive with chamfered dressings contrasting with a well maintained timber door. Glazing bars are missing on the ground floor windows. Sir Hudson Low (in charge of Napoleon at St Helena) is reputed to have lived here at the beginning of his military career.

No 9 The Parade   EOD

Kilkenny Design Workshops B

These 2 storey Gibbsian buildings when built around 1780 formed extensive stables for the Castle opposite. Since 1965 they have been occupied by the Kilkenny Design Workshops, a Government sponsored body which promotes good design in Irish industry. The conversion was undertaken by the architect Niall Montgomery and the builder was W. K. Cleere, Kilkenny.

The stone facade originally featured a blind arcade beside the pedimented coach entrance, the ground floor of which is of chamfered ashlar. The blind arcade has now been opened to provide windows. The central area is flanked by a slightly advanced facade of 5 bays in random rubble with dressings to the windows and a central blind coach entrance with Gibbsian surround pierced by a door. The entire facade is linked by a heavy Roman Doric cornice with mutules and balustrade. Above the pediment is a fine timber cupola with copper roof.

Internally the ground floor (with plaster ceilings) comprised stalls for the horses, with more meagre quarters over (without ceilings) for the grooms. Behind the front building is a semi-circular courtyard which is backed by curved stabling. All the first floor windows looking into this courtyard are circular (occuli) and pierced by four 'keystones' containing a timber glazed frame resembling the wheel of a coach.

The Courtyard, Kilkenny Design Workshops GD

East Side

From the Castle to the Imperial Hotel is a high wall pierced by an entrance to the formal Castle gardens. In front of this wall is a walk, known as Gravel or Mayors Walk fronted by railings and a line of trees — extensively pruned in 1975. The walk contains a utilitarian public lavatory. At its northern end is a limestone drinking trough which was commissioned from Mr Colles by the Kilkenny Society for the Prevention of Cruelty to Animals in 1902 at a cost of €58.5.0.

Kilkenny Castle   AH
See page 19, Section 1.

CASTLE ROAD

This road was constructed and, presumably, planted with trees by Walter Butler, 16th Earl of Ormonde in 1769 at his own expense. It runs south from the Castle gate and turns sharply at Switzir's Almshouse to join the Bennettsbridge Road, which formerly ran straight through the present Castle Park to the south wall of the Castle. The trees lining the road have reached maturity and are being replaced as they become decayed. It is hoped that similar replacements will take place on other tree-lined entrances to the city such as the Callan and Castlecomer roads so that such enhancement of the approaches by our forebears will be passed on to our descendants.

St James Asylum   B

Founded in 1803 by James Switzir. The Almshouse provided for 20 females in reduced circumstances (12 were to be Protestant and 8 Catholic). Switzir advertised in Finns Leinster Journal on 30th April, 1803 for carpenters, slaters and plasterers to work on the building. The Asylum consists of a terrace of 5 two-storey houses, each of 3 bays, with a clock pediment over the central house and facing across an enclosed lawn. The houses all have fanlighted doors and sash windows with all glazing bars intact. The handless clock face is of stone with incised Roman numerals.

The impressive entrance is at right angles to the Almshouse and consists of a fine pair of forged iron gates flanked by piers topped with an urn, a pair of wicket gate openings (one only remaining) and a pair of blind arches surmounted by a bracketed pediment. Within the eastern pediment is incised 'Dedicated to St James the Just' and in the other 'Founded and Endowed by James Switzir AD 1803'. Two plaques are beside the blind arches: one restates the latter while the other 'St James Asylum'.

At the far end of the Almshouses in an end wall parallel to the entrance is a niche which contains a statue of the founder. The complex is situated at the end of the Castle Road in a position of the utmost visual importance.

PATRICK STREET

Patrick Street is mainly a residential street much favoured by the professions. It leads from the Parade junction (which was formerly known as Croker's Cross from a memorial cross which stood in its centre) to the Waterford Road, through the former St Patrick's Gate. St Patrick's Church was originally sited outside the Gate. Only the graveyard of the original church remains. Long gardens behind the houses on the west side of Lower Patrick Street terminated at the city wall.

As the houses on this street are taken over by business concerns the facades should be retained.

East Side. Nos 1 and 2

Probate Office and Social Service Office. A large horizontal beam was discovered in No 2 some years ago during alterations suggesting a former use as a shop. The windows have been unsympathetically altered.

No 3   S

McGrath. A well maintained and attractive 3 storey 3 bay shop front with good lettering. The facia is supported by 4 Roman Doric engaged columns. The windows retain their glazing bars.

Nos 5 – 10   B

To the casual glance this is a Georgian Terrace. However, some of the houses have Tudor features and this group is formed of 3 pairs of similar houses.

Nos 5, 6: A 3 storey rendered facade with chamfered quoins over a basement. 2 niches are set in the facade between the houses and stone string courses project slightly. The 3 chimneys are Tudor as are the basement windows. Steps lead up to the entrances and the building is fronted by a stone wall with shaped coping. During alterations in No 5 some years ago, a beam was discovered bearing the name Ferguson and the date 1747 — possibly the date of a former reconstruction. A Tudor fireplace in the basement of No 5 was removed in 1974 to Rothe House.

Nos 7, 8: This 3 storey building was erected by William Colles, proprietor of the Kilkenny Marble Works, in 1759. The stone entrance door surrounds feature large stone lintels (approximately 2 m long) with chamfered dressings. No 8 has a forged iron lamp holder in front of the fanlight and the windows retain their glazing bars.

Nos 9, 10: A fine pair of 3 storey houses with entrance doorcases which have Gibbsian surrounds. No 9 has a ground floor double window whereas there are 2 separate windows in No 10. The 2nd floor contains small windows with two 3 pane sashes and the first floor 6 pane sashes (as also has the ground floor of No 10).

South Eastern Health Board, Stathams Garage. While these buildings maintain the street line, they are out of proportion with the remainder of the street.

No 12   A

A very fine 3 storey 3 bay Georgian house with chamfered quoins and a slate hung gable which partially closes the view down the Ormonde Road. The brick facade has a relieving arch over a stone entrance door surround which has 2 Tuscan engaged columns with pateras. The seven steps up to the entrance, which are flanked by railings, project into the street. 2 cast iron plates on the facade read 'Patrick Street' and 'St John's Ward 1844'. There are two 3-light windows on the ground and first floor. The windows lack glazing bars and are topped by brick voussoirs.

No 3   GD

No 12   EOD

No 13   S
Like No 12 this house is visually important since it partially closes the view down Ormonde Road. It has a fine Georgian doorway flanked by 2 attached columns, and the lintel and surround to the fanlight is fluted and contains 4 pateras. The concreted facade is fronted by railings.

Nos 15 and 16, Butler House   C
Butler House. A dower house of the Earls of Ormonde. This beautiful house was probably re-built in the 1780's when Walter Butler, the 16th Earl, was carrying out extensive improvements on his property in this area. It is notable for its fine reception rooms and ornate plaster work.

The eighteenth century character of the building, which is most evident from the garden, carries a hint of an older structure beneath. The reception rooms end in bows with three tall windows in each bow. A fine cut stone portico fronts the building.

The Kilkenny Design Workshops acquired the property in 1972 and commenced extensive renovations.

The section projecting into the street flanked St Patrick's Gate until the turn of the century.

Site of St Patrick's Gate   H
This entrance gate to Kilkenny bridged the road at No 16 Patrick Street. The corresponding house on the north west side of the street was demolished in 1973 and its replacement built by the I.T.G.W.U. has a satisfactory scale and proportion.

Nos 18 and 19   S
This building was erected in the early nineteenth century and is in an important visual position on the corner of Patrick Street and Ormonde Road.

West Side: Nos 20 and 21   C
Two good residences over a basement which are fronted by railings, with cast iron decoration, and share a flight of 5 steps up to their entrances which are similar to the doorway of No 13 but are in niche-porches. Two cast iron plates on the side of No 20 read 'St Canice's Ward 1844' and 'Ormonde Road'. At one time these houses formed part of the Club House Hotel.

Club House Hotel   C
The two houses which form that part of the hotel which faces the street are divided by a rib vaulted coach entrance (with one octagonal spur stone). The facade of the hotel is pebbledashed in a heavy manner but the fine late nineteenth century cast iron canopy (which projects out over the Gibbsian doorcase and 5 limestone steps) and the forged iron railings add a touch of lightness and complement the internal character. The interior public rooms (the hall, bar, stairs and dining rooms) are particularly fine with decorated ceilings with period light fittings and furniture. Many Spy cartoons decorate the walls and assist in the creation of an atmosphere which is unsurpassed in the locality.

The hotel is essentially a Georgian building which was enlarged in 1892 by the annexation of the home of Mr Patrick Watters, Kilkenny Town Clerk, during the proprietorship of Mr Thomas Murphy. It was originally the headquarters of the Kilkenny Hunt Club, founded in 1797 by Sir John Power of Kilfane. The Club was converted into a hotel when the new Cork road was constructed, and opened its doors as 'The Hibernian Hotel and Fox Hunting Club' on 4th August 1817. The scene of many eventful happenings, notably the wild escapades which took place when the Hunt Club met twice yearly for a week's hunting and conviviality.

St Patrick's Gate, c. 1900   COC

The Club House and No 24   GT

The opening Meet of the Hunt Club, in November, at the Hotel was a notable event in Kilkenny until about 1960 when traffic problems forced its abandonment. The annual dinner has, however been revived by the present Master, Major Victor McCalmont.

Nos 24 and 25   C

Two good 3 storey Georgian houses whose entrances have Gibbsian surrounds. No 24, formerly occupied by the I.T.G.W.U., has recently been tastefully reconstructed except for the painting of the doorcase. It has a fine first floor cast iron balcony serving two windows.

Kilkenny Theatre   C

Kilkenny Theatre was one of a series of magnificent gifts to Kilkenny conferred by Capt The Hon Otway Cuffe, son of the 3rd Earl of Desart and his sister-in-law Ellen Bischoffsheim, eldest daughter of a London Jewish banker and widow of the 4th Earl. The collaboration of these two was fruitful for Kilkenny and lasted from 1899 to the death of Capt Cuffe in 1912. He supplied the initiative and ideas, she financed and helped carry out the ventures.

The Theatre was opened on 27th October, 1902. In her memoirs Lady Desart recalls, 'Kilkenny awoke one morning to find herself the actual possessor of a theatre with stage and green rooms all complete and, if it was not a gem like the one Kilkenny had been so justly proud of in the years between 1798 and 1820, still it was a useful playhouse, capable of seating between eight and nine hundred spectators'.

After the death of Lady Desart in 1933 the theatre was carried on by the Stallard family until 1962 when it finally closed its doors.

Many other ventures are attributable to the two philanthropists mentioned above. The Desart Hall, a community centre and dance hall was built behind the Theatre, opening on to New Street. It is now the property of the Diocese of Ossory. At Talbot's Inch, one and a half miles north of the city they inaugurated a woodwork factory (of which some excellent work can still be seen in the city), the Greenvale Woollen Mill with a village and community centre for its workers, and a hospital — Aut Even, now St John's Hospital.

The Countess of Desart was a member of the first Senate of 1922 and was the first woman to be admitted to the Freedom of the City of Kilkenny (1910).

No 27

United Dominion Trust. A modern infill building which, though it maintains the street and eaves line, is out of character with the rest of the street. The full width horizontal windows are the antithesis of the vertical emphasis which predominates.

No 28   S

Allied Irish Bank. Formerly the Provincial Bank, which came to the site in 1860. A 3 storey, 4 bay Georgian building remodelled in the nineteenth century with a rusticated ground floor, chamfered quoins, broken-bed pediments to the first floor windows, and a return to the cornice with a parapet above. This is a nineteenth century equivalent of the face lifts which are currently occurring in the city.

No 29   S

The 3 storey facade contains four full height pilasters with Corinthian capitals. The western portion has double windows on the first and second floors with moulded surrounds, while the eastern part has single windows.

No 30   S

Kilkenny Journal. A 3 storey 3 bay pebble-dashed facade over a basement fronted by railings which contain a boot scraper. The windows have stone sills and glazing bars. The arched passageway under the Kilkenny Journal sign is flanked by circular spur stones. This passageway formerly ran through to New Street and connected with a sallyport, or small opening in the town wall. In this lane stood the town house of the Senior branch of the Rothe family. The family joined the Wild Geese after 1690 and served with distinction in the Regiment of Rothe. A descendant was lady-in-waiting to Marie Antoinette. The house was very old when in 1790 it was used temporarily by Kilkenny College while the College was being built. It was taken down in 1817-18 and the three houses now standing there were built as a hotel, as it was hoped that the new Cork road would enter Kilkenny at this point.

Nos 31 and 32

No 31: A 3 storey 2 bay Georgian building fronted by a railing and arched lamp bracket. The glazing bars are retained. An example of an old building being successfully converted for commercial use.

No 32 is fronted by attractive low railings containing twisted uprights — an unusual feature.

Nos 33 and 34   C

Avonmore House. The Hibernian Bank until recently. A 1905 reconstruction incorporating an adjacent house to the north east, of the original mid-nineteenth century bank. This house, which extended over the lane way, was the home of Dr Hackett, friend and supporter of Charles Stewart Parnell, and of his gifted family, several of whom were to achieve fame in the field of literature.

The novelists Francis and Florence Hackett lived in the building which formerly occupied the site of No 34 and which extended over the adjacent land. See page 42.

No 26, formerly Kilkenny Theatre GD

Lamp bracket, No 31 EOD

Presbyterian Church EOD

ORMONDE ROAD

This fine, wide tree-lined entrance to the city, with its continuation, College Road, was constructed in 1817 to open up the south-western approach to the city. It leads from Patrick Street, cutting through the old town wall to join the Callan Road at Rose Hill.

South East Side: No 10 S

Ormonde House. A 3 storey 3 bay building with overhanging eaves. 5 steps lead up to the recessed door with a contorted fanlight over, and fluted columns beside the opening. A visually important building which acts as a visual stop to travellers approaching Kilkenny from Waterford. Originally a Glebe house.

Presbyterian Church A

A fine Church built in 1870 with a facade in the Hard-Gothic style. The centre of the composition is Perpendicular, with a Tudor arched door and window, and is flanked by Early English lancet windows. At the corners are diagonal buttresses topped by a pinnacle, as is the apex of the crenellated gable. This building is worthy of a preservation order.

Technical School C

A 2 storey building of snecked stone fronted by lawns, an excellent wall and entrance gates (made by McGloughlin, Dublin). Behind the wall are trees including two splendid copper beech.

Constructed as a model school during the educational experiment in non-denominational schools which took place in the middle of the nineteenth century. The experiment was not successful but the school continued as such into the present century. It was converted into the City Technical School in 1939.

Talbots Castle and City Wall H

See Section 2.

Nos 12 — 15 S

Nos 12 — 14 comprise a pleasant 2 storey terrace at an angle to the road, aligned to the old City Wall, and present a nice feeling of domesticity (owing to the scale, neat gardens and the brightly coloured canvas which is put over the front doors as protection from the sun) between the institutional solemnity of St Kierans and the Technical School. No 15, a larger 2 storey building, is in a visually important position.

North West Side: Talbot House S

A 2 storey 3 bay Georgian building with a good doorcase in a niche atop 5 steps with engaged Tuscan columns, a fluted lintel with pateras, and a fluted fanlight surround which is similar to the doorcase of 13 Patrick Street. Unfortunately the six pane sashes of the first floor are missing on the ground floor. The house is fronted by wall (coping stone sadly painted), railings and gas lamp holder.

St Kieran's College BF

Rose Hill Hotel GT

COLLEGE ROAD

St Patrick's Parish Church

Commenced in 1896 and completed in 1899 at a cost of £7,326. The facade presents a very good example of Hard-Gothic architecture in the Decorated Style, with high gabled campanile and angled turrets and buttresses. St Camillus' convent of the Sisters of St John of God is attached.

St Kieran's College   C

Diocesan Seminary for Ossory. The foundation stone of this very fine building was laid in 1836. Built in the Neo-Gothic style to the design of W. D. Butler of Dublin, who also designed St Mary's Cathedral, and added to on many occasions since — the west wing being constructed in the 1950s to the design of Simon Leonard of the firm of W. H. Byrne & Sons, Architects, Dublin, and built by Walsh Brothers, Dublin. The entire wing was faced with dressed stone taken from the old church of St Johns — thus helping to preserve the appearance of the original building. The Chapel contains some good stained glass.

The impressive entrance gates, which formerly adorned the Jenkinstown Estate, near Ballyragget, were added in 1941.

Rose Hill Hotel   C

A 2 storey half-hipped building built by the Kilkenny architect William Robertson for himself, probably in 1830. (A plaque on the North Facade bears the inscription 'W. R. 1830')

The principal facade, facing west, is of 3 bays and is dominated by a castellated porch with spirelets. It has on either side a slightly advanced gabled bay with ornate bargeboards which are worthy of maintenance. These 2 bays have three-light windows, slightly recessed, the upper ones being segmentally arched.

The northern facade, through which the

building is entered, is a single-bay projection from the main body of the building. The ground floor consists of a 3 bay wide arcade of ashlar with steps in the central bay leading to a doorcase in the western bay. Above is a castellated Gothick oriel window and to either side is a sash window with hood moulding.

A warm, personal and light hearted building which sadly has lost some of its surrounding trees. Formerly the house of Michael F. Murphy, a noted collector of antiques, who added the charming brass door furniture.

William Robertson (1770-1850) was probably trained in England where he exhibited in 1897-98. Later he received considerable government commissions including the new County Gaol in Kilkenny (1808) and the Courthouse, Parliament Street. He is recorded as negotiating with the Coade Ornamental Stone Factory in 1816 for a statue representing Justice, a figure of Hibernia, trophies, etc. He is also recorded as working on Orchardton, Kilkenny, and Gracefield Lodge, Queens County.

In 1825 he undertook the restoration of, and elaborate alterations to Kilkenny Castle at the request of the Marquess of Ormonde. An article illustrating this undertaking was submitted to the Kilkenny Archaeological Society in 1852 by his relative J. G. Robertson, also an architect, and appeared in the Society's Journal of that year. J. G. also published in 1851 a collection of views of houses and other scenic attractions in Co Kilkenny drawn by artists engaged by William 40 years earlier with a view to producing a topographical work on the antiquities of County Kilkenny.

William Robertson had lived in William Street, Kilkenny in the early 19th century. In this street he had built a Diocesan Hall, now No 4.

The Imperial Hotel EOD

ROSE INN STREET

Rose Inn Street was, traditionally, the street of the Inns. Inns such as the Rose, the Garter, The Wheatsheaf and The Bush flourished at different periods. Its charming curve probably follows the course of the moat surrounding the Castle on its way southward to St Patrick's Church. The street appears on old documents as Rozyn, so the name is probably older than the period of the Inns.

South Side: Imperial Hotel   S

A large four storey building (with a 3 storey extension down the street) which dominates this corner and the view down Patrick Street. The gound floor plasterwork imitates blockwork. The west facade was fronted by railings until recently. The scale and proportion of this facade contribute much to the local townscape.

Nos 11 and 10   S

Brett, Hairdresser and J. Brennan, Confectionery. Two pleasant shopfronts; the former has been poorly modernised following a fire. Both have an attractive facia with dentils and modillions to the cornice supported by 2 engaged Doric Columns (with 2 consoles on hollow pilasters in between) and 4 engaged columns respectively. The upper floors feature double windows with glazing bars to the third floor of No 10.

Nos 9 — 1   S

A group of 3 storey buildings with a common eaves-line but with a large amount of variation in the quality of the ground floors, Nos 5, 6 and 9 being out of character.

No 7, Mulhall, has a charming black and white shopfront.

No 4, O'Connell, formerly Sterlings Pharmaceutical Hall, is particularly fine with its brass ground floor sills and brass shields beside the entrance which are set off by the brown and black paintwork.

No 3, the Munster Express Office, is visually important in that it closes the view down St Kieran Street. The upper storey contains ornate stucco work with alternating 'pecked' and rusticated quoins, pedimented second floor windows, and a balustrade on the top. This building was possibly the Garter Inn in former times. It is reputed that pikes were made in the rear of the premises in 1798, being subsequently secreted in the Castle grounds, unknown to the Ormonds.

No 2, Molloy's Bakery, has a plain, well maintained facade. The shop front and interior were completed around 1920 by Mr Costello of William Street. The first floor windows have moulded surrounds with scrolled consoles atop moulded shells. A heavy cornice tops the facade.

No 1, has its upper floor windows framed as No 2. A visually important building, as it confronts the eye from Johns Bridge. Formerly it was a Travel Office and its business included the provision of tickets for emigrants.

North Side: Nos 34 — 31 S

No 33, M. R. Bourke lives up to its name 'The White House'. A 3 storey 3 bay building. The ground floor windows have (unpolished) brass sills and the sign-writing is particularly good.

No 31, (formerly Piert's Ladies Shop) is in a visually important position on the corner of St Kieran Street. The upper floors are pleasant with a row of small brackets to the cornice; elegant moulded surrounds to the windows — with glazing bars; and large stucco quoins.

Nos 30 — 28 S

A 3 storey group with some varied ground floor architecture.

No 30, A. & T. Piert, is on the corner of St Kieran Street and also flanks St Mary's steps (leading to St Mary's Lane), formerly known as St Mary's Style.

No 28, is unoccupied and its ground floor with an unusual door and curved plate glass windows should be retained. The upper floors have double windows with rusticated keystones.

Shee Alms House A

See Section 1.

Nos 26 and 25

A 2 storey building bordered by a passageway leading to St Mary's Lane.

Nos 24 and 23 S

A 3 storey building. No 24, J. L. Parsons, has a modernised ground floor but it is important visually in that it projects into the street. Formerly the Bush Inn, where Thomas Moore, the poet, proposed to Bessie Dyke, an actress, in 1817.

No 23, Fitzpatrick Jeweller, has a pleasant black shop front, with good gold and red lettering with 2 double windows above.

Rose Inn St GT

Nos 22 — 20 S

No 22 and 21, Griffin, has an excellent facade which is most attractively painted. No 22 has a first floor double window but the upper floors have new windows while No 21 has the 'original' windows. 'Griffin' at one time was written high up on the gable. The entrance is pleasant with R. Griffin formed in mosaic, with a good light above the door.

No 19 S

Thomas Bairéad, Chemist. A 4 storey building and the upper floors contain double windows with some original glazing; also there are windows high up in the gable wall. An interesting shopfront which contains some stained glass.

No 18 to corner

The Parade Supermarket and Lounge Bar (site of the eighteenth century Wheatsheaf Inn); White, Victualler; and Elliott, Foodmarket. Visually the most important group in Kilkenny as it faces up the Parade, but it contains some poor architecture.

Rose Inn St, from Mayor's Walk MF

Nos 6, 7 and 8 Horseleap Slip EOD

HORSELEAP SLIP

Runs from the end of the Rose Inn Street to the north. Veterinary Surgeons practised in this area in former times and horses were exercised here. The buildings which flank the west side are visually important as they confront those travelling over John's Bridge.

Nos 1 — 5 S

An attractive 3 storey group overlooking the River Nore. All the buildings in this row have vermiculated quoins, acanthus type decorations to the brackets on the facias, and moulded window surrounds with stops. At the south end of the group is an illuminated cigarette advertisement which damages the view.

No 2, Tynans Bar, is one of the best maintained premises in Kilkenny. Much attention has gone in to the conservation of the interior and exterior and this is much appricated by its patrons. The period facia is illuminated by concealed lighting; a good solution to the problem of illuminated signs.

No 3, formerly Royal Liver, features attractive moulded details on the windows and door with pleasant lettering. Unfortunately the ground floor is unoccupied.

No 5, is now derelict and the limestone paving stones to the front are worthy of note owing to their scarcity. Earlier in the century much of the city was similarly paved.

No 6 S

An attractive house in sad company. The first floor bay window is similar to those or 1 and 2 Canal Walk.

Willoughby's clock GD

CANAL WALK

Runs from Rose Inn Street to the south. The public lavatory and E.S.B. sub-station are unforgiveable and should be screened if possible.

Nos 1 and 2 S

A pleasant 3 storey 3 bay house with first floor bay windows to afford the occupants a better view.

Canal Lodge S

Built about 1850 by Dr Robert Cane of 8 William Street. He was elected Mayor for second time in 1849 and, to mark the occasion, gave this fine cut stone lodge to add to the dignity of the Canal Walk. The plaque was placed on it through the good offices of William Kenealy (Mayor 1873). In 1844 when Robert Cane was Mayor for the first time he gave the 2 fine chandeliers to the assembly room in the Tholsel. This lodge, recently very well restored, is now the workshop of Peter O'Donovan, silversmith. A gate way to Canal Walk was recently removed and the cast iron plaques from the piers are now in Rothe House.

HIGH STREET

The main street of the English town was built by the English settlers about 1200 to give access from the newly built Castle to St Canice's Cathedral. Previously traffic ran between St Canice's Cathedral and St Patrick's Church by St Kieran's Street and Rose Inn Street. As the main centre of commerce the houses have been constantly rebuilt but many of the foundations are of great antiquity. It leads into Parliament Street.

West Side: No 1 S

Willoughby, Jeweller. A fine 3 storied rendered building in a very important position with regard to the townscape, standing on one corner of the busiest junction in Kilkenny.

The 3 windows on the first and second floors have moulded surrounds and 2 pane sashes. The beautiful late Victorian shopfront with a pair of hollow pilasters at each end (with a door between the northern pair) is in excellent repair. The attractive gold leaf signwriting is regularly renewed using the original templates. The etched glass panes in the entrance door remain. The gable has a facia, with a strong cornice, supported by 4 hollow pilasters; the large 'Willoughby's clock' faces up Patrick Street from behind a window; above are 4 windows with moulded surrounds. A lamp bracket is on the corner.

No 2 S

Castle Bar. A 3 storey 2 bay building attractively sandwiched between its neighbours. Recently superfluous additions to the exterior have been removed to the betterment of the townscape. The interior has charm (the plastic excesses of other public house renovations being avoided) and the real beams can be seen in the ceiling of the bar.

No 3 C
Allied Irish Bank. Built in 1921-22 on the site of the Victoria Hotel which was renowned as a political gathering place. The Architect was Thomas Scully and the Contractor was Hearne & Son, Waterford.

A soild stone facade typical of the period. The new plastic sign is out of character but the interior has been restored with great sensitivity preserving all the best features.

Nos 4 — 9 S
No 4, Tylers, is a 4 storey building. Above the first floor is the raised Art Nouveau lettered slogan 'Tylers Boots Are The Best' and above the 2nd floor in raised lettering 'Ormonde House'. 'Tylers' in ornate lettering is written on the gable in line with the roof pitch. The Ormonde Alms House was erected here in 1631 and removed for the present building in 1840. John Hogan, writer, historian, carried on his business as a painter, decorator and auctioneer here at the end of the last century. A door with a Gibbsian surround is to the rear.

Nos 5 and 6, Marlow Cleaners & Mulhalls, are in a 3 storey building. The former has 2 dormer windows above and the former attractive shopfront (Godwin) replaced by unnecessarily large plate glass windows. The latter has a black and white shopfront — the facia topping 5 hollow pilasters of which 3 have consoles with foliage decoration supporting the cornice — with a nice mosaic threshold reading 'Electricity Supply Board' in copperplate lettering.

Nos 7, 8 and 9, Quality Shoes, Tholsel Bar and Reynolds, occupy a 4 storey building each of 3 bays. No 8 has an unsympathetic ground floor while the upper floor windows have moulded surrounds with stops. No 9, visually important since it projects into the High Street, is on the site of the Old City Gaol. Beside No 9 is an entrance to Pudding Lane. Note the spur stones.

Nos 10 and 11 C
FitzMaurice, J. Murphy. One of the most attractive groups in the city. This 3 storey 6 bay building, with oak beamed cellars, appears as the White Hart Inn on a map drawn by James Healy in 1816 but originated much earlier as the 3 hood mouldings on the gable overlooking Friary Street indicate.

No 10 has a really dignified 19th century facade, painted black and white, with a spur stone beside. The full width facia, bearing the name FitzMaurice in severe Roman lettering, is supported by 2 pairs of attached Doric columns with a common pedestal. The 3 well proportioned first floor windows, with moulded surrounds and 6 rectangular pane sashes, have heavy stucco pediments supported by consoles. The second floor has 3 windows with moulded surrounds each with cornice and consoles. A balustrade tops the building above a heavy cornice with mutules.

No 11 has 7 pilasters supporting the facia. The first and second floor windows have glazing bars, moulded surrounds, and decorated keystones. The unusual green facade has 'Woollen Hall' in red raised lettering above the first floor.

Nos 12 — 15 S
No 12, Lenehans, is a 4 storey building topped by a heavy cornice and 10 brackets; consoles and cornice to the first and second floor windows; the modern facia badly obtrudes on the first floor windows; an attractive tapered octagonal stone wheel guard with heavy iron rail is on the corner with Friary Street. The southern gable is pierced by 5 windows.

No 15, Bourkes and Curtain Design. The former has a pleasant little shopfront with 4 attractive cast iron fretted grilles beneath.

Nos 10 and 11 GT

No 16 S

Bradbury. A 3 storey building with a vaulted entrance beside, leading to the Hole in the Wall. Over the entrance is a window with 6 pane sashes and a hollow pilastered aedicule. Over the modern shopfront (with illuminated projecting sign) is a 3 light window with glazing bars and aedicule.

The second floor window is similar except for the removal of the aedicule. The roof unusually has crest tiles with trefoil piercings. A visually important building which closes the view up St Mary's Lane.

The Hole in the Wall H

See page 38. A 16th century building of which some gables, chimneys, walls and windows remain. It may have been part of the Archer Mansion though it is directly behind No 16.

Nos 17 – 19 SH

O'Connor, Lawlor, Doherty. The Archer family mansion bearing on the street facade the date 1582 and the armorial bearings of Martin Archer.

Most of its octagonal chimney stack was recently removed for preservation in Rothe House. Alterations revealed cut stone 16th century doorways within the house. The rear portion retains some Tudor features and had until recently the remains of a formal Tudor garden. More recent occupants were Reverend John Francis Shearman, antiquarian and historian, Thomas McDonagh and Francis Sheehy-Skeffington, 1901-1903.

The 4 storey facade contains recent single pane sashes. Some moulded surrounds, with pateras, remain on No 19.

Two interesting shopfronts flank an unusually wide doorway (in possibly a Tudor opening). O'Connors shopfront features hollow pilasters with raised lozenge moulding altered to permit the addition of show cases. Above the segmental arched fanlight is a cornice, with modillions, which extends over Dohertys, supported by 2 unmatched brackets. Beside the doorway (flanked by 2 pairs of pilasters) is a Model 120 cast iron bootscraper made by A. Kendrick & Sons. The facia of No 19 is supported by 2 Roman Doric engaged columns. A most humorous ground floor illustrating the vernacular traits of the Irish craftsman which should be preserved.

No 20

Hibernian Insurance. This 4 storey building forms one side of Post Office Square and maintains the roofline, but it is an insensitive piece of modern architecture when viewed frontally.

No 21 CH

Mrs Purcells. This is a really fine 3 storey Georgian house with an elegant doorway and windows on the upper storey. It was not always rendered, the quality of the stonework at the rear is excellent and should be even better on the front. There is a stone cornice with a separate iron gutter supported on brackets. This is a feature of Kilkenny's Georgian buildings. The square is fronted by forged iron railings with an arch containing a lamp bracket.

Nos 22 and 23 S

Mahony's Chemist. This forms the other side of the Post Office Square, fronts the High Street and forms one corner of William Street. A stained glass Art Nouveau side entrance door has contemporary fittings. The modern shopfront hides the first floor sills. The upper floors have nice double windows with bracketed cornices and pateras. A former owner was P. M. Egan author of 'A Guide to Kilkenny'.

Nos 17 and 19, The Archer House GD

High St from Tholsel GD

Tholsel Arcade O

No 24   S
The Monster House. A 3 storey building with an 8 bay rendered facade. The ground floor windows are of plate glass, some of them being curved. The handsome facia sign of 1903 which has been restored was probably the work of the Countess of Desart's woodwork factory at Talbot's Inch. The entrance features a superb threshold of multi-coloured mosaic, the finest in South East of Ireland incorporating the name of the shop. It should be preserved.

Nos 25 and 26   S
T. M. Mooney, M. A. White. A 4 storey 18th century building of 3 and 2 bays respectively. Both premises have excellent Edwardian shopfronts, unfortunately obstructing the first floor sills, with good signwriting which should be retained. No 25 retains the glazing bars in all windows and the scale of the panes is echoed by the cast iron filigree work on the facia. The archway to Guard Lane runs under Mooneys which contains a cast iron cover inscribed John Young and Sons, Kilkenny, a pleasing detail which emphasises the individuality of the town. The facade of No 25 is spoilt by projecting signs. 'Maison Philomena' on a raised panel above the first floor of No 26 has recently been painted out.

No 27   C
The Ulster Bank. The bank acquired this site (which formerly contained a Birch house) in 1911 and the architects were Blackwood and Jury. A splendid 3 storey building with Poyntz Lane running under one of the 4 bays. The ground floor is of dragged finish limestone with 4 polished limestone engaged columns (Tuscan shafts with Ionic capitals) of poor proportions. The upper floors are of brick with stone quoins with paired windows with stone surrounds. The southern half of the building is topped with a blind balustrade; the northern half features an advanced gabled wall facing the street with broken bed pediment with egg and dart moulding containing a circular window above an armorial device with rampant lions and a shield. The brick chimneys have oversailing courses. The curious alignment of the Bank is possibly connected with the Old Market Cross which was formerly situated in the locality.

Nos 28 and 29   S
O'Carroll. A 3 storey 5 bay building with parapeted facade with O'Carrolls and Ormond Cleaners shop on the ground floor. These projecting shop fronts smother the central entrance door and mar a fine building. The first and second floor windows (6 pane sashes) have moulded surrounds with raised cornice which enliven the facade.

'China Glass O'Carroll Wallpaper Paints' is attractively written on the facade and 'Wedding Gifts' on the gable. The interior contains a splendid staircase.

Nos 30 — 32   S
Nos 30 and 31 were formerly the Scotch House.

A 3 storey group which, while not having any noteworthy features, does maintain the scale of the street in marked contrast to the buildings to the north.

One bay of Sherwoods contains the entrance to Colliers Lane, indicated by a cast iron plaque, which could be accentuated by the removal of plaster on the arch.

The former L & N shop is attractively faced with brown ceramic tiles, contrasting white woodwork and incised gold lettering on the facia.

O'Neills has an interesting roof and return over the arch into Chapel Lane. This arched entrance contains 5 spur stones on the northern side to protect the wall from the hubs of cart wheels — a common feature which should be retained. To the rear of this building was found in 1894 the Kyteler memorial stone dated 1280, now in St Canice's Cathedral.

Nos 34 and 35
The Kilkenny People, Delehanty. Modern architecture of a poor order, totally unsympathetic to the street with no effort to maintain eaves line or the scale of the buildings opposite and to the south. The entire premises, originally all Delehanty's Hardware Shop, was destroyed by fire in 1946.

This area of High Street is the site of an early Norman Church and, in the sixteenth century, the residence of Sir Richard Shee which was taken over in Cromwellian times for the headquarters of the notorious Governor Axtell. Ecclesiastical and Tudor domestic remains have been found here, some surviving numerous fires and finally being demolished in the disastrous fire of 1946.

Nos 36 — 40
Formerly Smithwicks, Murphys and Potters. The fine 4 storey premises of D. Smithwick & Co, fronted by a row of 4 limestone steps (as originally was Delahuntys) to compensate for the fall in the street, was cruelly destroyed by fire in 1970. The ancient premises of Potters, when demolished, contained the longest period shopfront in Kilkenny. During the redevelopment a thirteenth century beam with dog-tooth ornament and a nineteenth century stained glass display window were salvaged and placed in Rothe House.

The modern replacements have a scale which is not in keeping with the overall character of the street.

Between 38 and 39 is Red Lane, now a cul-de-sac but formerly connecting High Street with the sconce or passageway of the Town Wall.

Nos 41 — 43   S
MacEneaney, Murphy, Rothe Inn. 3 storey premises of which the only feature of note is the charming front of Murphy's bar and variation in pitch of roof from No 41 to No 42. Murphy's cosy interior is typical of the smaller bars in Kilkenny. Beautiful porcelain and brass beer pulls, rods on the wall and fine talk of fish and fishing.

No 44   S
The Metropole Hotel. The hotel and No 43 flank James Street and create a void which has a sympathetic scale. A 3 storey building, with glazing bars to the first and second floor windows, which was formerly the Munster & Leinster Bank and earlier still a police barracks.

No 45   S
John Gunn. A 3 storey single bay building with a double window on the first floor and glazing bars to the window above, with an attractive shopfront.

East Side
The group of buildings from the Pembroke Bar to the south is important for the character it imparts to the street and, indirectly, the town. As individual elements they are of little consequence but their summation is of the utmost consequence — especially in

The Market Cross   ROC

view of the poor streetscape opposite. Their value derives from their scale; their proportions — they are taller than wide and in general their individual parts (the pilasters, the columns, the doors, the windows) complement the proportions; their warmth — which only small businesses can generate; their pleasant variation in roof height; their delicate tones which accentuate their individuality. Any unsympathetic alterations to the individual elements not only affect that element but the whole group.

In this area, the visitor no less than the surveyor will find the numbering of the buildings confusing. This is because the street has been re-numbered on at least three occasions and some premises have retained an earlier numeration.

Nos 50 — 52   S

T. Dore, The Country Shop. A 3 storey building which is a visual stop to Parliament Street and frames the entrance to High Street and Kieran Street. The pavement is really well-handled on the corner.

No 52 has an attractive shop front with 3 hollow pilasters, acanthus leaf consoles to the facia, and gold lettering. The first floor window has a moulded surround with decorated keystone and, unusually, 8 pane sashes. The second floor has a window with an 8 and a 4 pane sash.

No 53   S

The Old Curiosity Shop. A 3 storey building with the gable facing the street. The facia has modillions to the cornice. A plaque on the facade says that the street was founded in 1200 and widened in 1883 when John Hogan was Mayor. Stone quoins are evident where the rendering has fallen away.

No 66   EOD

Nos 54 — 57   H

The Shambles. A walled-in area for the slaughter of cattle was erected here at a very early date and remained until the end of the last century — probably removed when the street was widened in 1883.

Pembroke Bar to O.K. House   S

The Pembroke Bar. A pleasant 3 storey 2 bay building with moulded surrounds to the windows (and keystones on the first floor) and stucco quoins. The bar has good signwriting on the facia and an attractive interior — fitted out in mahogany by Parnalls of Narrow Wine Street, Bristol. Until about 80 years ago a butchers shop, as evidenced by the socket for the butchers rail inside the window.

Set into the facade is Barry, Greengrocer, which is probably the smallest shop in Kilkenny. This shop visually links the scale of the Shambles with the larger building to the south.

Singer: This shop has sold sewing machines since the turn of the century and beside it is the Market Slip through to Kieran Street. These slips are one of the most attractive features of the town and should be maintained and improved with the addition of, for example, lighting in character. The survival of the slips depends on the maintenance of the buildings beside them.

St Joseph's Dry Cleaners: Demonstrates how a weak or spoiled shopfront may be supported within a terrace, provided the same basic proportions are maintained. The company slogan 'St Josephs — above all others' is interesting. It used to be a butchers, fronted with an open iron grille. When the Public Health Act declared open fronts insanitary, the grille, together with much fine ironwork in the town disappeared.

The O.K. House: Established by the Griffins in 1926, it has a pleasant black shop front with gold lettering.

No 66   C

The Marble City Bar: A 4 storey 2 bay building with a brick facade which is higher than its neighbours but fits into the street owing to its pitched roof. The ground floor front with its two terminating engaged columns, hollow pilasters with heavy consoles, and fanlighted door painted red, and a black facia with incised gold lettering is a good example of the Edwardian period. A schedule of fittings written in 1908 reads: 'Swing doors of mahogany and plate glass, window railings and gates, four side screens, two marble topped counters, one set of mirror-backed bar fittings, two earthenware wash-up stands with waste pipes, one plated muller, three marble-topped tables, one set of continuous cane-backed seating, one six-jet brass gas rail, three gas chandeliers, one six-pull beer pump with pipes attached'. The bar, like the Pembroke, was fitted out by Parnalls of Bristol. Around 1950, it was closed for two years through lack of custom!

Nos 65 — 63   S

Three 4 storey premises which have a common eaves line with stone cornice and separate gutter on brackets (as No 21 High Street). No 65, Browne, has good signwriting on the facia. No 64, Ger Doherty, has an attractive ground floor with blind by Nolan & Son, Dublin, and signwriting by John J. Fitzgerald of the highest calibre. The trend to plastic facias is to be deplored and unless the trend is halted, the signwriting craft could die out. Inconspicuous flood lighting is available which would both illuminate the facia and facade and permit the craft to continue. Such a solution should be encouraged.

No 63, St Canice's Credit Union, has an unsympathetic ground floor but does maintain the former facia height.

Burton and the Gas Company   SH

A 3 storey 5 bay building. These two shops constituted one of the town mansions of the Shee Family. Built about 1600 it extends to St Kieran Street where the Shee escutcheon is still visible. The Burton shop (formerly Hipps) has an ornamental Tudor chimney piece surmounted by the Shee arms. The first motor garage in Kilkenny was established here by Messrs Statham around 1903.

Ryan — Healy   S

Between G. L. Ryan and Healy part of a seventeenth century gable can be seen.

Post Office

A building which tends to be more conspicuous than necessary through not having a pitched roof (which the other tall building in the vicinity — The Marble City Bar — does have) and by having a first floor balcony and flag pole. However, the windows on the upper floors have good proportions which permits a degree of harmony with its neighbours.

Francis Doheny (a local solicitor) threw a brick through a window of the old Post Office here around 1900 and declared a one-man republic — immortalised in a play by Denis Johnston, 'The Golden Cuckoo'.

Nos 74 — 78

This stretch of 3 storey shops though constantly being altered, retain bits of their ancient character. Some shop fronts have been unsympathetically modernised, such as No 76. No 77, O'Connor, until recently, had an attractive bow window. A cut stone window dating from the sixteenth century was recently uncovered in No 76.

The upper storeys have a nice unity although it is a pity that windows with a horizontal emphasis have been put into the upper floors of No 74 and 77.

Nos 79 — 82   SH

J. Bourke. A pleasant 3 storey 4 bay building which is visually linked to its neighbours to the north by a moulded surround to a sign area between the first and second floors. On Bourke's this area exhibits the good lettering 'General Drapers and Outfitters'. The shop slogan 'Worth Will tell' is depicted on the facade in neon and above the entrance door. The threshold has 'Bourke and Sons' in brown mosaics on a white ground.

A. D. Finnamore and Lanigan and Nolan, Solicitors. A 3 storey 5 bay building of lower height than No 79. The former has an attractive ground floor flanked by fluted engaged columns. The latter has a black ground floor, with threshold below pavement level, which gives the small entrance a certain dignity.

Beneath the northern bay is the arched entrance to the Butter Slip. Potentially the most attractive of the Slips linking High Street and Kieran Street and a real effort should be made to conserve it. The Kilkenny Amenity Study prepared in 1970 by the Architectural Students at the Bolton Street College of Technology, Dublin, showed how this could be done. The buildings enclosing the Slip contain portions of stone doorcases and mediaeval stone windows.

No 82   H

A 4 storey 2 bay building, with an ugly blind to the first floor window. The house of Edward Rothe, nephew of Bishop David Rothe and probably the house in which the latter died. A Tudor fireplace was removed from the rear in 1973 and is preserved in Rothe House, Parliament Street.

The Tholsel GD

The Arms of Kilkenny. These armorial bearings, with the addition of a spire on the central tower, were ratified by the Chief Herald of Ireland at Dublin Castle in January 1976 EOD

The Tholsel B

This interesting building consisting of a double arcade, five arches in length, with Council Chamber overhead, is crowned by a steeply pitched hipped roof and lantern clock tower. It was rebuilt in 1761 at a cost of £1,315. The architect is unknown but a persistent tradition attributes the design to Italian origins and there are very similar buildings in Northern Italian towns such as Florence which are still used for the same purpose as Kilkenny Tholsel, *viz* as a market place. Kilkenny Tholsel, as well as being the seat of taxes had booths on the street floor until early in the 20th century.

In 1759 Sir William Evans Morres and three other members of the Corporation were empowered to oversee the rebuilding "agreeable to the moddell in wood this day produced at the board . . . and pursuant to the resolutions of this day that they or any three of them do ornament the same both without and within in such manner as in their judgement shall be meet and fitting . . ." according to the minutes of the Corporation of the 20th February of that year.

The arms of Kilkenny were carved on the south facade around 1820 by the Colles family. This blazon was the version accepted in the 18th century. Earlier versions varied but the three turreted castle is common to all.

The Council Chamber is a beautifully proportioned room and unmistakably Georgian. In mediaeval times this area of High Street was an open space in which a Market Cross was erected in 1335 but removed in 1771.

Under the architect W.O. Morrissey, Carlow, part of the building, notably the stairs, was reconstructed in 1951.

O' Keefe S

A large facade rendered in an uninteresting manner in an important position flanking the Tholsel. The large raised lettering echoes the size of the shop. An attractive doorcase with fanlight is to the rear of the shop in St Mary's Lane.

Nos 84-86 S

The premises of P.T. Murphy (Jeweller) and No 86 form a 3 storey 6 bay group. Murphy's shop front is exceptionally good and the black paint sets off the merchandise — echoed by the fine lettering. This shop sign was made and signed by the Kilkenny Woodworkers around 1903. Nos 84 & 85 have a painted brick facade with voussoirs to the windows; a cornice with the gutter carried separately on long arm brackets. When the roller shutter on the ground floor is lowered and the sun shines across the facade, it has an excellent textural quality. Rendering to No 86 and alterations to the eaves make it dull in comparison.

The Corner House S

A 4 storey single bay building defining the entrance to St Mary's Lane with first floor three part window (unusual for Kilkenny) while on the second and third floors are double windows.

High St towards the Parade c. 1910 NL

Nos 84 and 85 MQ

Nos 88 and 89 S

W. H. Good. A 4 storey building with a 2 bay facade on High Street in a visually important position since it projects into the High Street and is on the corner of St Mary's Lane. The Mary's Lane facade contains a fanlighted opening (formerly a door and now a show case) which closes the view down the lane, and a shop front with heavy cornice and well proportioned lettering which practically closes the view up the High Street. Above this shop front, the name 'Good' is written vertically down the facade and makes it all the more interesting.

The High Street facade has a ground floor shop front with 5 hollow pilasters (the down pipe is ingeniously set in the northern pilaster) and the third floor retains the glazing bars in its sash windows. The retention of glazing bars on the East side of the street is unusual and here (in white on a well maintained brown painted facade) they make the building more lively.

M. O'Connell shares the same building and the results of insensitive modernisation and poor maintenance can be clearly seen.

Woolworth and Crotty H

Until around 1928 this was one of the finest buildings in the town; an Elizabethan house potentially as good as Rothe House which was altered by Woolworths despite protests from many Kilkenny citizens. It was the town house of Henry Shee, Mayor of Kilkenny in 1601 and 1611. His arms, impaling those of his wife, are sculptured on a stone slab set in the wall. Beneath is the inscription 'Henry Shee of Kilken; Gentleman and Francis Crisp, his wife's armes'. The date, said to be 1580, is broken off.

Nos 95 and 96 S

Allen's has a modernised ground floor; the 19th century upper storeys are particularly fine with the window surrounds, quoins, (alternately rusticated) and dentils painted in a contrasting colour. The stepped roofscape to the rear adds interest.

No 96, Farrell, is dull in comparison.

Nos 97 and 98 S

No 97, Frank Wall: A painted brick facade with voussoirs to the windows. The facia contains good signwriting.

No 98, Ryan: A shopfront of the type that is gradually disappearing and being replaced by large areas of plate glass and aluminium or Neo-Georgian. There are few painted woodgrain doors remaining and this is one of them, set to the rear of a pleasant mosaic threshold.

No 99 — corner S

An important group of buildings owing to its position at the principal junction in Kilkenny, although the alterations carried out to the group do not maintain the High Street's traditional character.

No 99, a 3 storey building with a hipped roof projects out into the street and is visually important.

The block from White, Chemist, to White, Victualler, in Rose Inn Street formed the offices of the Kilkenny Journal 1830-1902.

Formerly this corner was known as Crokers Corner on account of Crokers Cross which stood in the centre of the street here and called after John Croker, Sovereign of Kilkenny, in the early fifteenth century. No description or illustration of the Cross is known.

FRIARY STREET

A very old street known as Walkin Street until quite recently. Up to 1817 this was the main entrance to the city from the south west (Cork Road) and had a gate known as the Walkin Gate. The origin of the name is uncertain. It may be the Walking Street leading to the Walking Green, or Walkin may have been the name of a very early owner. The former Upper Walkin Street is now named Walkin Street.

North Side: Nos 1—6

An undistinguished group. Beside which is a car park which, with its wall of different coloured brick and gloomy evergreen tree, is an example of the way the motor car is affecting our town centres. The 1970 Kilkenny Amenity Survey used this area for residential purposes.

Nos 17, 18 S

These two houses (of 3 and 2 storeys respectively) flank the laneway known as 'The Walkin Street Sconce' or 'Garden Row'. They define the laneway in a lively way with their rusticated quoins and moulded surrounds with rusticated stops and it is important to retain them. No 18 has a moulded cast iron gutter.

South Side: Nos 31 — 44

Mainly a group of 2 storey buildings. No 44, a 3 storey eighteenth century house with 2 three-part windows on the ground floor with glazing bars to all windows, bears a plaque on the wall recording the death of two patriots during the War of Independence.

The town wall crossed the street at this point. The Gate known as Walkin Street Gate was mentioned as early as 1305 and removed around 1809. A row of houses (since removed) was built on the site of the wall and was called Garden Row.

No 40, a 2 storey 3 bay building, has its original six pane sashes on all but one window and has great charm — indicating the warmth the street had in former times and which is barely lingering on. Opposite a manhole cover bears the inscription 'Kilkenny Main Drainage 1930. Shannon Foundry Limerick. J. G. Duggan Mayor'.

PENNEFEATHER LANE

Runs at the rear of the Capuchin Friary between the church and Friar's Garden down to Pudding Lane. The lane was constructed around 1700 by John Pennefeather, a local land owner, and then known as Penney Lane. Originally it had 20 dwellings down either side.

Capuchin Friary

The Capuchins first came to Kilkenny during the Confederate period. They had many houses during the eighteenth century when they led a fugitive existence.

In 1848 the present church was built on the site of Father Tobin's Poor House. During the years since many additions and alterations have been made. The portion of the church running parallel with Friary Street was completed in 1874.

Doorcase No 4 GT

WILLIAM STREET

Leads off the High Street opposite the Tholsel. Many of the buildings are of a high architectural quality. The street widens at the end into a little square and a narrow exit — visually closed by a pleasant doorway — links with Garden Row. The views up and down the street have superb visual stops. This is Kilkenny townscape at its best.

Prior to 1800, when it was much rebuilt, the street was known as Boltons Lane. Around 1900 at the S.E. corner of the street was the premises of P. M. Egan, Bookseller and Newsagent. P. M. Egan, author himself, and Mayor of Kilkenny in 1887 and 1888, was the father of Milo Egan (born here in 1895), the dramatist and author of 'The Dominant Sex', a successful play.

South Side: Nos 2 and 3   S

Two pleasant 3 storey 2 bay houses over a basement. No 2 has casement windows while No 3 retains its 6 pane sashes on the lower floors and its 6 pane and 3 pane sashes on the second floor.

No 4   C

A 4 bay 2 storey house with a stone arched coach entrance in the fourth bay. The building is fronted by railings on a low stone wall with a shaped coping. It has a magnificent wide doorcase with engaged Tuscan columns, entablature with mutules and a fine fanlight. The house was built prior to 1825 by William Robertson as a diocesan hall.

Nos 5 — 8   S

An excellent 3 storey group each of 2 bays, except No 8, over a basement and fronted by railings with integral footscrapers. The stone doorcases are all similar except No 8 which is set in a niche; No 7 has a gas lamp holder mounted on the wall. Glazing bars are retained throughout.

No 8 is a 5 bay building with an arched coach entrance in the fifth bay. In 1849 the owner, Dr Robert Cane, had Thomas Carlyle as his house guest. The latter tells the story of his visit in his 'Irish Journey'. The former was founder member of the Kilkenny Archaeological Society in 1849 and its first Hon. Treasurer. He died in 1858 when the house became the home of the Potter family.

Nos 9 and 10   S

Two 3 storey 2 bay buildings with glazing bars. In the western gable of No 10 are 5 windows, which attractively break up the wall, including a window with 9 pane sashes.

The Manse House   S

A 3 storey 3 bay house flanking the Methodist Chapel. There are 2 two-light windows with 4 pane sashes to the ground floor, 2 two-light (4 pane sashes) and a single light window (6 pane sashes) to the first floor, and three windows to the second floor. Unusually for such a house, there is a timber doorcase with fanlight.

Chapel   S

A rough faced ashlar building with the pedimented gable front rendered and containing 3 tall round headed windows — the central one over the entrance with timber doorcase.

The Rev John Wesley, founder of Methodism, first visited Kilkenny in 1756 and the first church was built in 1771. This was superseded in 1802 by another in William Street and it in turn was superseded by the present building.

No 11

Regent Cinema. In the early years of the century Clerys had an important coach making factory here. A fine cut stone arch was adjacent until the advent of the cinema in 1948.

No 12 C

An important 3 storey 3 bay building of rendered random rubble which closes the view down the street. A similar facade to the Manse House, it is fronted by a wall and railings. The timber doorcase has a fine stone portico with fluted engaged columns to the rectangular columns. The entablature contains mutules and the shallow arch beneath has a patera in the spandrel. The rear wall has weatherslating.

The passageway between the cinema and No 12 is visually closed by a timber doorcase flanked by wheelguards.

North Side: Nos 13 — 15 S

A 3 storey terrace with simple narrow doorways with moulded surrounds and a pediment above a pulvinated frieze. There are double windows on the first and second floors and in No 13 the glazing bars have been retained. Uncoursed rubble with segmentally arched brick voussoirs to the windows in the rear walls.

No 12 GT

Nos 17 and 18 S

The C.Y.M.S. In the nineteenth century this was the premises of the Citizens Club. John Banim attended many functions here and in 1835 was presented with a silver snuff box and a purse of sovereigns. In 1848 the Young Irelanders swarmed up the street and were addressed from the windows by John Blake Dillon and William Smith O'Brien.

Nos 19 — 21 S

A 3 storey group each of 3 bays with casement windows except for the ground floor of No 19 which retains its sashes. No 21 is considered to have been the Swan Inn in the eighteenth century. No 16 is similar to the houses in this group.

Monster House

An extensive frontage to William Street well painted in a neutral tone with raised lettering picked out in white. Four ground floor windows have ornate cast iron guards and spice the elevation.

**CHAPEL LANE &
WELLINGTON SQUARE**

This area of the city has great potential as it is one of the few lanes on this side of the High Street which still has a residential population. Commercial life has invaded the eastern part of the lane and this should be prevented from spreading towards Wellington Square. The Square itself is most pleasant and affords a good view of St Mary's Cathedral. At one time the old James' Street chapel (built between 1772 and 1774) stood nearby. A plaque commemorating the Chapel used to be on a wall near the Square but is now on a wall of Our Lady of Fair Love School.

A section of the old Town Wall borders the passageway from Wellington Square to James' Street.

The spatial qualities of this open area, in contrast to the confines of the lane, could be improved by paving, the planting of deciduous trees, and the removal of the ESB pole and the plethora of wires. This area merits a preservation order.

South Side: Nos 8 — 12 S

A pleasant 2 storey terrace of good scale. Nos 8 and 9, 10 and 11 have double doorways in an arched recess with a fanlight over each door. Nos 10, 11 and 12 have double windows on the first floor. In general the glazing bars have been retained to the windows. Beside No 12 is an area which would be suitable for an infill building. The rears of these houses, viewed from Collier's Lane, are attractive with a pleasant mixture of brick and stone, and tall round headed windows to the staircases.

Rear No 8 Wellington Sq, and Chapel Lane GD

Nos 5 — 7 S

A group on the west side of the square each of 3 storeys with 2 bays similar to Nos 1 — 4. Nos 6 and 7 share a double doorway the unity of which has been upset by the addition of ironwork to No 6. No 5 has a hipped roof.

North Side

The school building at the western end presents a monotonous facade of grimy grey pebble dash to the street. Yet the building has good windows with stone sills, and with suitable painting would entirely complement the buildings opposite.

Nos 13, 14 and 1 — 4 S

A 3 storey group with basements beneath Nos 1 — 4. Nos 13 and 14 have 3 light windows on the first floor and the sash windows retain their glazing bars. Nos 1 — 4 have charming double doors, in an arched recess, separated by a hollow pilaster, with good fanlights. These doorcases are similar to Nos 8 — 12 but have superior fanlights.

Chapel Lane and Nos 8 and 9 Wellington Sq GD

St Mary's Cathedral BF

Cottages in Cathedral Square GD

JAMES STREET

Runs from High Street to St Mary's Cathedral. The view down the street is closed by the Shambles with the Johnswell Hills in the background. Signs and wires should not detract from this view.

South Side: Nos 5 – 10

A 2 storey group with Nos 5, 6 and 7 having a double window on the ground floor.

Convent

The Presentation Convent presents a boring facade to the street which is relieved by two unusual brick framed openings and an incised stone reading 'Convent National School 1860'.

North Side: Store

Above the Metropole Hotel is a store built in random rubble with brick dressings to the openings. The openings, which are mostly filled in, suggest that this building was formerly a terrace of houses. Unfortunately it is in poor condition but it does give some feeling of warmth to this street and relieves the coldness of the adjacent metal gate. The building used to belong to Sullivans Brewery (see St James Sconce, page 73) and was used as a mineral water store. It probably ceased being used for this purpose when Smithwicks took over Sullivans around 1917.

St Mary's Cathedral   C

St Mary's Cathedral was built on the plan of Gloucester Cathedral of the best Kilkenny limestone (from the Black Quarry). Begun in 1843, it was consecrated in 1857. Its fine tower is the most conspicuous building in Kilkenny and is seen clearly from all approaches to the City. The Victorian altars and furnishings are all fine examples of their time. The best statue is of Our Lady by Benzoni, an Italian artist, and the Sacred Heart altar was constructed by the Pearse family of 1916 fame. The stained glass is German. The Cathedral plate includes 17th century chalices presented by the Archer, Butler, Langton and Bryan families.

The most unusual tomb in the Church is to Mr Michael Desmonde, a mural tomb of Renaissance style. The Potters, Cullens, Fennessys and the Hylands are the only other families to be buried within the Cathedral.

In the Cathedral Close the presbytery of finely cut limestone was erected in 1864 and the Chapter House about 1890.

Cathedral Square

The Square is principally a car park for worshippers but is often sullied by the presence of commercial vehicles. The row of cottages (architects — John Thompson & Partners) on the east side is a commendable lesson in scale and the use of indigenous materials. Hopefully the houses which are being removed near the south transept of the Black Abbey will be replaced by buildings of a similar scale and so permit the dominating presence of the south window to be appreciated by future generations.

The Maltings GD

Evans Lane and Brennans Forge GD

JAMES SCONCE

Leads from James Street to Evans Lane. A pleasant lane of superb contrast, the industrial building and the domestic cottages, linked together by a curving stone wall.

The 'Sconces' were originally narrow passageways inside the city walls which gave access to the defenders of the city.

East Side: The Maltings   C

A magnificent 3 storey industrial building of squared rubble with brick dressings to the openings. At the northern end is a fine spur stone with a stone corbel above. The view of the building is marred by an ESB pole with 21 wires attached.

The Civil Survey of 1656 records 'A malthouse on the West side of High Street standing backward in James Street'. This was the property of James Bryan and is thought to have stood on the site of the present Maltings.

In 1810 William Sullivan in partnership with Mr Loughnan bought the James Street Maltings from the Archdekin family and it was to remain in the Sullivan family until 1917 when taken over by E. Smithwick and Sons who use it still as a Maltings.

The principal member of the Sullivan family was Richard Sullivan, died 1855, who was MP for the city on two occasions, and held all chief municipal offices during his life. Sullivans, Brewers and Maltster Manufacturers, were established in 1702.

To the north of the Maltings is the facade of a domestic building which is worth restoration. Adjacent to it is a fine cut stone archway and a random stone wall which sadly has been lowered at the top of Evans Lane. Why are such walls treated so callously?

West Side

Opposite the stone wall are two charming cottages with heavy brick chimneys (Nos 3 and 4) which are fronted by a narrow pavement with stone kerbing. No 5, which deserves maintenance, is beside a badly sited ESB pole.

EVANS LANE

Leads from Parliament Street to St James Sconce. A sympathetic observer standing at the top of the lane will readily see this lane's potential. There are good views of St Canice's Cathedral, the Johnswell Hills and the lane narrows leading the eye to the manifold pleasant additions, alterations, and materials at the rear of the Parliament Street premises. Further down the street Tudor remains are clearly visible.

The lane has not been lined with large commercial buildings like many others and the several derelict stone buildings could be imaginatively converted into flats, etc. Unsympathetic modern buildings and garages are a slur on its former dignity (as evidenced by the unique cut stone doorway in the premises of J. O'Reilly) and future potential.

JAMES GREEN

This is a pretty square of rendered stone built houses dominated by the Catholic Cathedral. The railings and wall around the Green are rather ugly and the square would be improved by their removal. Some seats might be provided and deciduous trees planted. The Green was originally used for bull baiting; a statue of the Virgin now stands in the centre. This statue, an example of Italian mass produced 'art', is one of two statues erected during the Marian Year, 1954. The other, a madonna, by Seamus Murphy R.H.A. (1905-1975) was commissioned by the workers of Kilkenny Woollen Mills, Greenvale, and is now in the grounds of the Retreat House, Sion Road. This beautiful piece of sculpture is worth a visit.

Nos 1 — 7, 8 — 16, 20 — 28 S

Terraces on the south, west and north sides respectively. Nos 14 and 15 are sadly derelict and should be renovated. Nos 12 and 13 provide the best examples of the original condition of the houses. Any renewal or improvements to the houses should maintain the scale and character of the existing buildings.

Seamus Murphy's Madonna, Sion Road TB

Old shop front, St Mary's Lane GT

Former doorway GT

PARNELL STREET

Connects James Green and James Street with Friary Street. Formerly called Flood Street after Henry Flood who owned property in the locality.

Nos 1 — 26 S

A pleasant 2 storey terrace with stone sills on the west side of the street fronted by small gardens, a low wall and railings. Three cast iron plaques state 'Founded 1888 by the Corporation. P. M. Egan, Mayor 1887-1888'.

Nos 1 & 2 have their original six pane sashes but others like No 3 have been modernised.

Byrnes Store

This steel framed, metal clad building erected in 1975 is a visual incongruity and the environs of a cathedral should be free of commercial enterprise.

ST MARY'S LANE

From High Street (between Goods and Kellys) this lane goes round 3 sides of St Mary's Church — the fourth side being bounded by St Kieran Street. The lane has two very pleasant qualities; a spatial mystique which derives from the many curves, corners and steps; and tranquillity as one passes from High Street to Rose Inn Street or St Kieran Street. Any alterations in the lane should maintain its character and these qualities.

An old shop front, with hollow pilasters, and matching fanlighted door to the rear of O'Keefe, and a former doorway with fanlight in the side of W. H. Good close two views in the lane superbly and should be maintained.

Shee Alms House CH
See page 21. The adjacent extension over the lane is totally out of character with the surroundings. The goods entrance to the west has been badly executed.

St. Mary's Church B
See page 23. It is unfortunate that the environs of the Church are used as a car park. Grass and benches would be welcomed by shoppers and shop assistants at lunchtime.

St Mary's Alms House C
Founded by Rev Peter Roe, Rector of St Mary's, around 1840. Rev Roe (1777-1841) was a noted preacher and benefactor of the poor. He preached charity sermons in Kilkenny, Dublin, Liverpool and elsewhere in order to raise money to build Almshouses.

A 3 storey 5 bay building in random rubble with a hipped roof with overhang. The window voussoirs and quoins are of dressed stone. The second and fourth bays are slightly advanced and pedimented and until relatively recently were doorless. Basic skills in stone cutting and stone masonry are displayed here and have been effectively handled by the architect. C.f. the rendered Evans Home in John Street which has stone work of a much higher order.

Nos 9 and 10 Kieran's St EOD

KIERAN'S STREET
Leads from Parliament Street to Rose Inn Street and was named after St Kieran's Well and site of an ancient church at the northern end. It was probably the oldest route leading from St Canices to the monastic settlement at St Patricks. Successively named Low Lane, Back Lane, King Street and Kieran Street. The southern end developed as a craftsmen's area, a characteristic it retained well into the twentieth century. The west side of the northern end consisted of the rear facades of mediaeval High Street houses while on the eastern side a row of fine residences faced the street with long gardens and orchards at the rear extending to the river. It was fashionable in the eighteenth century to add a summerhouse beside the river bank. The east side is scheduled for redevelopment — Oh! How are the mighty fallen!

East Side: Molloy's House
A most commendable new house. The design is clean and unfussy and relates in a no-nonsense fashion to the street with its paving and simple railings.

Nos 8 — 10 S
An interesting terrace of 3 two storey houses, which have been associated with craftsmen. No 9 was the home of Joseph Hackett, silversmith, watch and clockmaker. No 10, the home of John Smith, upholsterer. No 9 retains the glazing bars on the first floor. No 10 is the most attractive house with matching architraves around all the windows and the door. The ground floor architraves originally probably contained 3 light windows.

No 11   S

Ryan and Power, Dentists. Formerly a vet's house, the garden leading to Horseleap A good 3 storey 3 bay house, with basement, with a limestone step to the door. It retains its glazing bars and has windows high in the gable wall. The house is fronted by a low stone wall surmounted by railings.

Nos 12 and 13   C

Two fine eighteenth century brick facades which should be preserved. The main feature is a good double doorway (n.b. variation in fluting on the friezes) topped by a brick relieving arch, which appears to be from the same hand as the excellent doorway of 88 and 89 John Street. The houses have 4 storeys over a basement; the ground floor of No 13 has been rendered all over, while a large ground floor window has been inserted in No 12. Unfortunately, these houses appear in need of maintenance. No 13 was formerly the house of William Ireland, an umbrella mender who also kept lodgers.

No 14   S

Callaghan and Connolly is painted on the fanlight over the entrance door (with a Gibbsian surround) which is atop two steps. A 3 storey 3 bay eighteenth century facade with segmental arches over the first floor windows. If one stands on the opposite side of the road twenty-two electricity wires can be counted leading to, or in front of, the house.

Kieran's St towards Castle   GD

No 17   S

Hennessy and Young. A fascinating single storey facade (with basement) with three dormer windows, with shaped barge boards in the roof. The full width facia is terminated with brackets featuring acanthus leaf decoration.

Sixteenth or early seventeenth century chimneys with dressed quoins with rubble infill. Five limestone steps to the door flanked by octagonal bollards. The entrance adjoining leads to Butlers Yard and Corcoran's (panel beaters). Butler was a coal and timber merchant here in 1839. The three storey house (possibly seventeenth century) to the rear of No 17 is interesting with an exceptional vernacular stone doorcase featuring a lintel with 4 lozenges containing a stylized flower in relief. The uprights have a patera in the centre with a recessed panel above and below. The lintel is flanked by a palmette in relief and topped by a heavy cornice. The building is scheduled for demolition but every effort should be made to save it or its principal features.

The streetscape from No 17 to the south is very lively with great variety in the fenestration, eaves line, roofscape; in weight from delicate pateras to massive stacks; and in texture.

Callaghan and Connolly Store

A 3 storey building with an entrance, dividing the premises to the rear, and a peaceful overgrown garden. A piece of sixteenth century carved stone is employed as a spur stone at the entrance!

Nos 20 and 21 S
A pair of 3 storey houses of uncoursed rubble over a basement with three stone steps (plus an attractive forged footscraper) up to a double doorway topped by a basket arch. This building is similar to those on the south side of Chapel Lane.

No 22 S
'Working Men's Club Est. 1886' reads the raised capital on the facade. An epitaph should be added 'and destroyed 1975'. This 3 storey house over a basement was lived in in the eighteenth century by a solicitor, a doctor and later a tailor. It contains a fine pine staircase and a huge carved flamboyant fireplace surround.

Nos 23 and 23A C
A 3 storey house over a basement with steps up to the two entrance doors which are 1.5 metres above pavement level. The building appears to be early eighteenth century and the ground and first floor contain three-part windows. Wrought iron railings front the building.

Wool Store S
'C. J. Mulcahy Wool Store' reads the yellow lettering with white edging on a green background, over the entrance door. A 3 storey building with a first floor door with a projecting hoist bar. Old glazing bars in the upper floors.

Kyteler's Inn SH
A strong tradition identifies this house as the home of Alice Kyteler, the moneylender and reputed witch of the 14th century. Known as Kyteler's Hall in 1449, it later became an Inn. It was handsomely restored in 1966 by the architect Colm O'Cochlain. How much, if any, of the present building dates to the 14th century is conjectural. The vaulting of the ground floor below street level may be compared with parts of Bishop de Ledrede's Palace built about 1354. In both cases the remainder of the buildings belong to the 18th century. The Inn was in the hands of a member of the Shee family in the early 17th century and was probably also rebuilt then, as many of the remaining cut-stone windows are of that period. East of the house in the court yard is the Well of St Ciaran — a clear bubbling stream surrounded by masonry. This was a church site (presumably St Ciaran's Church) pre-dating the Norman conquest and apparently attached to the monastic establishment of St Cainneach. It was handed over to the Earl Marshall before 1200 to enable him to extend his town of Kilkenny and then it disappears from the records. In the basin of the well was discovered a beautiful thirteenth century fluted baptismal font (now in St Francis Abbey) similar to those in St Canice's Cathedral and St Mary's Church.

In the 18th century the church ground became the garden of Kyteler's Inn which extended as far as the river bank and probably boasted a 'tea house' on the river as neighbouring houses did.

Nos 28 and 29 S
No 28 is A & M Jackson. Apparently an old building with a sixteenth or early seventeenth century window in the gable wall. The architraves to two second floor windows have rusticated stops. There are stone footings to the entrance door (which formerly must have been grander) with a nice mosaic threshold inside. The gable wall contains a pier which supported a pair of gates leading to the Market Yard. A pair of these gates, reputedly the finest gates made in the city (by the Downes brothers who emigrated to the U.S.A. afterwards), are unhappily stored in the Corporation Market Yard and could perhaps be erected at the entrance to Canal Walk or Johns Quay Walk.

Nos 30 and 31 S
Daniel W. Bollard's Lounge Bar. A robust facade with the entablature (bearing the number and proprietor's name) 'supported' by eight square pilasters and terminated by consoles supporting a ball. Each window architrave contains two bracket stops with acanthus decoration. This two storey building with slate hung dormer windows to the front and rear has rusticated quoins. A well maintained building with appropriate colouring.

West Side
Commonly called 'Slips Side'.

Corner to Market Slip
A mixture of 2, 3 and 4 storey buildings (formerly part of the old Shambles) with, apparently, a delightful Georgian shop front at the southern end. In fact, the shop is the remains of a film set for 'Lock Up Your Daughters' (from the restoration comedy by George Farquaher, who was possibly educated at Kilkenny College) made in 1968.

At the top of the 20 steps at the Market Slip on the north wall can be discerned (just) the following:

'Any person found committing nuisance in this laneway will be prosecuted. By order of the Sanitary Authority'.

Open stalls were set up by butchers in this slip to sell veal and tripe to people going to the market.

Callaghan & Connolly Store S
A 3 storey 3 bay building (possibly seventeenth century) with dormer windows. The first floor contains two double windows and a plaque bearing the Shee Alms. On the store south gable is a projecting chimney, supported by five stone corbels, and a built up stone window surround. This store was formerly the rear of Elias Shee's House which extended back from the High Street.

Nos 39 and 40   S

No 39, Dick Brett, Hairdresser. A 2 storey 2 bay building. Pleasant red, cream and green painted signwriting enlivens this part of the street. Glazing bars to the first floor windows. No 40 is a similar building.

J. Healy

Iron Store. A 4 storey gable. This building was formerly Cantwell's Iron Store and this store traditionally supplied many of the local blacksmiths. The present premises of Healys (formerly a Langton house) are divided by the 22 steps of the Butter Slip.

No 43

Murray. An attractive visually important 2 storey building, with hipped roof, which projects into the street and is flanked by 16 steps leading to St Mary's Lane. The keystones to the door architraves depict oak leaves and acorns. Good signwriting on raised panels.

No 49 to Rose Inn Street   S

These buildings maintain the street line. The 3 storeyed No 49 is being renovated. Nos 50, 51 and 52 belong to Molloy's bakery and like the rest of Molloy's premises are well maintained. This building white with red woodwork. The last building, No 53, is a 3 storey building and is on the site of a building John Rothe had next to St Mary's Steps in Kieran Street before he built Rothe House. It was the Parochial School in 1871. The concreted facade includes five hood mouldings and a stone plaque bearing the date 1818.

Rear of Shee House, Kieran's St   GT

PARLIAMENT STREET

Runs from High Street to the Watergate and Irishtown. It was incorporated into Englishtown before 1218. Named after the Confederate Parliament of 1641-8, it was earlier called the Coal Market.

Here, as elsewhere, telegraph poles disturb the eye and assault the day-dreaming pedestrian. Fortunately the ESB has undertaken to put the wires underground in the city centre by 1980.

West Side: Nos 1, 2 and 3

V.G. Supermarket. A modern 2 storey building which represents what is poorest in modern design. There has been no attempt to follow the eaves line of the adjacent buildings or to harmonise with the existing character of the street. Formerly a sixteenth century building which was demolished in the early 1960s. A Shee coat of arms which was on No 1 is now in private hands. Stallards shop, which stood on this site, was one of the last shops in Kilkenny to shutter its display windows at night and maintained the old custom of putting up one shutter when a funeral was passing. A sixteenth century chamfered stone window surround was salvaged when the supermarket was built and is in the courtyard of Rothe House.

Nos 4 — 6

A 4 storey building with a string course to the second and third floors which acts as sills to the windows. The facias obstruct the first floor sills.

No 7   C

A 3 storey 3 bay rendered facade well restored. Limestone steps, with railings, at right angles to the facade rise to a simple fanlighted door. The ground and first floor windows have 6 pane sashes, with 3 and 6 pane sashes on the second floor.

The lane between 7 and 8 was traditionally known as Jesuit Lane. Probably originally a right of way to the James Street Sconce, or Wall Walk. The Jesuit Order is known to have been active in Kilkenny after the Reformation.

Nos 8 — 13   S

These are good buildings which contribute to the varied and dignified character of the street. No 8, Moore, has an unsympathetically modernised ground floor but fortunately retains the plate glass curved windows. The 3 storey facade is topped by a parapet and heavy cornice.

No 9 has been recently modernised. The good proportions of the building are marred by the ground floor.

Parliament St, c.1910 NL

The "New Building" GT

No 10, Lennon, has a 4 storey 3 bay brick facade. The attractive ground floor contains 5 engaged Doric columns and the facia's signwriting echoes the classicism of the columns (c.f. No 10, High Street). The facia contains a sun blind — a feature slowly disappearing. The first, second and third floor windows have heavy moulded surrounds with cornices to the first floor windows. The gutter is carried on long arm brackets.

No 11, Grocer, a 2 bay 3 storey facade with a three light window to the first floor.

No 12, McCreery, contains an out-of-character ground floor, the facia of which obstructs the first floor sills.

No 13, T. Foley (The Hibernian House) is a large 4 storey 4 bay building which retains the glazing bars to the upper windows. As elsewhere the upper floors are spoilt by an illuminated projecting sign. The gable has traces of weatherslating. Evans Lane runs under the fourth bay.

No 14   S

R. Wall. A 2 storey building whose character is accentuated by its size in relation to the mass of its neighbours. A charming ground floor with 2 well worn limestone steps to the door. Formerly the 18th century Eagle Inn which survived as a hostelry until this century.

Rothe House   AHS
See Section 1

Nos 17 and 18   S
These buildings were built later than Rothe House. No 17, John Murtagh, is a 2 storey building with vermiculated stucco quoins and aedicules to the first floor windows.

The facia unites the 4 pilasters and 2 doors below while the brass sill to the window bears the inscription 'Dispensing Chemist, Perfumer'. Good period door furniture.

New Building Lane passes under the fourth bay, and is named after the fine house on the north side of the lane of which only the facade remains, containing fine cut stone early 18th century windows, door and traces of pilasters (or similar).

No 18, Eltone Cleaners and formerly DeLoughrey, is an attractive building with dormer windows above the second floor and a well-decorated ground floor with stone quoins at the southern end. Six pane sashes to the first floor windows show what the windows of No 17 were formerly like. Formerly DeLoughrey's Foundry (1816-1965). To the rear stands the gable of a Tudor house traditionally associated with the Jesuits. The brickwork and asymmetrical openings at the rear of this group provides warmth and charm.

Peter DeLoughrey, the father-in-law of the present owner, Mrs C. DeLoughrey, while imprisoned in Lincoln Jail made a key within the Jail in order to permit the escape of Eamon de Valera.

Nos 19 — 21
The southern end of the facade of No 19 is at an angle to the street. The only glazing bars in this group are in the third floor of No 20.

No 22
Crotty's Loading Bay. Regrettably, this ugly concrete facade replaced a beautiful classical brick house erected by the Rothe family.

Crotty's Bakery   C
A magnificent 3 storey 3 bay building with superb stonework and gauged brickwork, erected in 1903 for T. Crotty by Carbery, Carlow. The massive stone facia, with incised gilded lettering, is supported by 5 limestone chamfer rusticated piers topped with capitals. The first and second floors are of red brick with stone quoins and contain window openings topped with segmental arches dressed with round-nose bricks. Modillions support a heavy cornice and the building is topped with a grey brick chimney.

At the northern end is a 2 storey 'extension'. The ground floor contains a similar facia supported by brick piers and stone capitals. On the first floor is a Venetian window with stone shields above. A heavy cornice is supported on brackets. Pierced crest tiles to the ridge.

No 22 and the bakery   GT

The building is carried through into Abbey Street where the craftsmanship is of the same standard.

No 24   S
Conway. A visually important 3 storey 2 bay building which defines the entrance to Abbey Street.

Nos 25 — 30   S
A curving group of buildings gently falling away to the Breagagh river with varying pitches to the roofs — fine vernacular townscape. The curve lures one to look further while the monopolistic concentration of licensed premises tempts one to linger!

The facade of No 25 and 26, The Silver Birch, contains a dull modernised ground floor while retaining a pleasant interior. Above are two two-light windows with moulded surrounds and decorated keystones.

No 27 is a similar building.

Abbey St 1965   COC

No 28, Tallent, has a pleasant ground floor with good three-dimensional signwriting.

No 29, The Sportsmans Inn, has an entablature added to the first floor windows and a bracketed string course at second floor sill height.

No 30, Phelan, has a 3 bay 3 storey facade with a spur stone lined passage in the third bay. A cast iron plaque bears 'Parliament Street'.

East Side: No 31   S
James Hughes. A 2 storey rendered building in an important position since it visually closes the southern end of Watergate.

No 34 S

A 3 storey 2 bay rendered facade over a basement. Fronted by a telegraph pole radiating 26 wires and a low wall with railings. Glazing bars to first and second floor windows.

To the north of this building a car park permits one a view of the brewery. This area will require sensitive planning in the future to echo the character of the buildings opposite and define the street line.

Nos 35 and 36 S

Two fine Georgian 2 bay 3 storey buildings over a basement, terminating an attractive group running to the Courthouse, fronted by a low stone wall with moulded stone coping and railing. Chamfered stone quoins to the north and south. The gutter is carried on long arm brackets in 2 styles. Appropriate painting would make this a most attractive pair.

No 35 has 3 limestone steps to the door which has a stone doorcase, with fanlight. The interesting 'lintel' has a 3 part keystone which is both structural and decorative. First floor windows have 6 pane sashes and the second floor windows 3 pane sashes.

No 36 is similar to its neighbour but features a 3 part window on the ground floor with hollow mullions. Slate hung gable. Was a Police Barracks during the Black and Tan era.

No 37 S

S. McGrath. A low 3 storey 3 bay building which is older than Nos 35 & 36. The ground floor has a well maintained shopfront with good signwriting. The first floor windows have 6 pane sashes and the two second floor windows have 2 pane sashes.

Nos 42 and 43 GD

Nos 38 and 39 S

A 3 storey 5 bay building. An old building which has subsequently been 'Georgianised'. To the rear are the remains of the Red Lion Inn of which they may have been a part. Some Tudor openings remain.

Nos 40 and 41 C

Two really fine Georgian houses, which merit a preservation order, each with a 4 storey 2 bay brick parapeted facade over a basement. Fronted by a low wall with railings and integral bootscraper. Three steps lead up to the fine double doorway with its 3 engaged Tuscan columns, fluted entablature with five pateras, and wide fanlight topped by a brick relieving arch. (The doorway is similar to Nos 88, 89 John Street and should be compared with No 12, 13 Kieran Street.) The glazing bars are retained on the second and third floors. The facade is in need of decoration.

Nos 42 and 43 C

Another fine pair of Georgian houses. Each has a 3 storey 3 bay facade over a basement but the first floor sills to No 43 are slightly higher. No 42 has six pane sashes on the ground and first floors and 3 pane sashes on the second floor. The two adjacent doors, with Gibbsian surrounds and original fanlights, are fronted by three steps and a low wall with railings and integral bootscrapers. Chamfered quoins delineate the facade. The rear of these houses is of stone with brick surrounds to the windows and presents an unusual roofscape. The gutters are carried on long arm brackets.

No 43 extends to the South over Jenkins Lane, which emerges in Watergate as Horse Barrack Lane.

This right of way passes through an area formerly known as the Bull Ring, now occupied by Smithwicks Brewery. The archway has a brick groined vault and is fronted by a fine stone arch above which is a good new sign (replacing a plastic one) identifying the brewery. The setted surface of Jenkins Lane is noteworthy and should be preserved. The doorway at the bottom of the Lane has unique iron hinges.

No 44 S

A 3 storey 4 bay building similar to Crotty's Bakery opposite. The channelled ashlar ground floor contains 3 round headed doors and one window. Above is a stone string course on brackets above which is a gauged brick facade. The 4 first floor round headed windows have stone keystones and above is a string course. The second floor windows have segmentally headed openings. The composition is topped with a cornice on brackets and edged with stone quoins alternatively vermiculated.

The Courthouse B

The present County Courthouse, re-built and altered many times over the centuries was originally the site of the town house, or castle of the influential Anglo-Norman family of Grace. It still retains the secondary title 'Grace's Oldcastle'. It was yielded to the Crown for use as a 'Sheire Gaol' in 1566 by James Grace, and presumably rebuilt. James was rewarded by being appointed Constable, or Governor, of the Goal and was given an income of 20 nobles a year.

The date of its conversion into a courthouse is uncertain, but it must have been sometime between 1758, when a contemporary town plan shows it still marked 'County Gaol' and 1792, when the first recorded sittings of the Assize Court took place in it. However, it continued to retain some of the features of a prison, and still does, as the cells which are visible at street level vividly attest. Citizens still living remember part of it being used as a Bridewell or lock-up.

Conversion to the purposes of a courthouse must have required further substantial alterations, possibly to the designs of one Sir Jerome Fitzpatrick, who is recorded as having visited Kilkenny in 1792 and to 'have proposed some plans of material service to the courthouse which will be immediately carried into effect'. Its present dignified and coherent effect, which accords well with the streetscape, can be attributed to the architect William Robertson, who, about 1830, remodelled the facade and added the balcony and stone staircase.

Internally, only the well-proportioned main hall with its barrelled ceiling remains as Robertson left it. The two court chambers, with their quaint furnishings and wooden balconies, and their massive docks with steps leading directly down to the cells below, fell victims to the ravages of dry-rot and had to be completely renewed in recent years.

And so, for close on 200 years, this building has been the seat of the law (if not always of justice!) in Kilkenny.

The facade of the Courthouse is marred by inappropriately sited street furniture and the partition of the forecourt.

No 46 S

Crotty, Solicitor. A 3 storey 2 bay rendered facade over a basement which is important because it preserves the street line and frames the Courthouse.

Market Entrance H

The site of the Old Parliament House which is commemorated by the lower of the two plaques on the southern entrance pillar. The upper plaque reads 'Public Markets. Established under 24th Victoria Chap 49. Alexander Colles Esq. Mayor 1862 and 1863'. Between these pillars hung a magnificent pair of forged iron gates which were made by the two Downes brothers. Reputedly the finest gates ever made in Kilkenny, the Downes were paid so little for them that they emigrated to America. The gates sadly lie neglected in the Corporation Stores.

Teahouse S

At the bottom of the Market Yard beside the Nore, are two buildings. The southern one is particularly attractive and has been dated to the eighteenth century. Owing to its position in what was then a garden possibly of the Shee family, it was probably a teahouse — tea being a fashionable drink at the time.

Bank of Ireland

An insensitive example of concrete expressionism which has regrettably replaced a superb mid-nineteenth century building and, with Winstons beside it and the VG Supermarket opposite, detracts from the character of the town.

The Courthouse in 1861 KC

Watergate GT

Irishtown towards St Canices EOD

WATERGATE

A charming little curved street of miniature shops which marked the spot where the jurisdiction of the Mayor ended and that of the Portrieve of Irishtown began. The little river Breagagh which runs beneath, was the dividing line and the gate to the Hightown was above the bridge. Alas, Watergate has recently lost its eastern shops, much to its detriment.

The Mayor now rules both the Hightown and the Irishtown.

West Side: No 1   S
Abbey Bar. A 3 storey 2 bay rendered facade.

Nos 2 and 3   S
No 2 has a 2 storey 2 bay facade with dormer windows.

No 3, Hickey, is 2 storey and has 3 bays. These two premises with openings in slightly odd positions, add charm and interest to the area.

No 4   S
Doherty. A 2 storey 2 bay facade with dormer windows and an attractive black painted shop front. The facia, with heavy cornice, is terminated by consoles and supported by two pairs of fluted engaged columns with a door between each pair.

No 5
A 2 storey 2 bay facade with a ground floor shop.

Nos 6 and 7
A 3 storey building with the facade height as No 4 resulting in a compressed second floor. The gable acts as a visual stop to Irishtown. Beside No 7 is the Breagagh river. The west wall of the bridge contains an old raised stucco panel containing the incised legend 'Post no bills'. Let us remember its creator for a job well done and sparing us from election posters etc.

No 9 GT

East Side

Until recently here stood a terrace of pleasant shops which were demolished to serve the internal combustion engine. Now the Kilkenny citizen is faced with tarmacadam, ugly bollards, a blank gable and not even a view of the river and the attractive double arched stone wall of the bridge. Replace the wall with some of the old railings which are stored by the Corporation, pierce the gable with windows to echo those at the far end of Irishtown, replace the tarmacadam with paving, plant an indigenous tree.

IRISHTOWN

Irishtown has few good buildings but is undaunted by the towering presence of St Canice's. It can offer the citizen every facility. It has bustle and character. It has telegraph wires and projecting signs too, which detract from the view of St Canice's.

West Side: Nos 1 — 3

A 2 storey heavily stuccoed facade in need of maintenance. The three chimneys have heavy cornices.

No 1 has pierced crest tiles to the roof. Beside it is an attractively carved stone pier which acts as a memorial to the stoneworking family of Hoban — whose descendants are now in the U.S.A.

Nos 4 & 5

A 2 storey building with the upper floor containing three-light windows. No 4 was formerly Irishtown Post Office and retains a pleasant ground floor and G.R. pillar box.

Nos 6 and 7

A 2 storey building. The shopfronts of Nos 5 and 6 are garishly adorned with signs.

No 8

A 3 storey 3 bay facade in poor condition. The upper floors retain sash windows with glazing bars.

No 9   C

Formerly Apparelle. The building is unusual in that the gable fronts Irishtown and is of 3 storeys and 3 bays. Until recently it contained an excellent Georgian shop front with original glazing bars to the windows. The present windows are typical of the phoney 'Georgian' windows now being installed throughout the city, and the illuminated signs are in the poorest taste.

The corner of the building bears the following plaques 'Irishtown', 'Dean Street', 'St Canice's Ward 1844', and 'Arthur McMahon Mayor 1877'. The threat of demolition for road widening, which hung over this vitally situated building, has mercifully receded. Its restoration (including the insertion of dormer windows) began in 1975 and doubtless it will now witness the demise of the motor car.

East Side: No 10

Walsh. A 2 storey 2 bay facade to Irishtown with a hipped roof. It has an unattractive projecting facia. It acts as a visual stop to Dean Street.

Nos 11 and 12

Treacy, Garage. A 3 storey building of 3 bays each. The upper floors are good with moulded surrounds to the windows; the first floor sills have been destroyed. The ground floor compares unfavourably with the human scale of Nos 13 — 16.

Nos 13 — 16   S

A pleasant 2 storey group.

No 14, The Veg. Shop, has a charming ground floor.

No 16 was formerly the premises of Kelly Coachbuilder as the raised ornate lettering on the facia indicates. The ground floor has 9 half fluted pilasters and a heavy cornice. Compare the coachbuilder with its successor the motor garage to the north.

Nos 17 and 18

J. Lowry. A 3 storey 6 bay facade with stops to all the window surrounds. The ugly ground floor hides the first floor sills. A good north gable of coursed rubble. The south gable would benefit from piering by well proportioned windows echoing those of No 1 Dean Street.

DEAN STREET

This street leading west and south-west towards Kennyswell, had an entrance to the Dean's residence before the construction of the Coach Road. The Dean's Gate to the Cathedral precincts was probably situated in its narrowest area.

South Side:
St Canice's Widow Asylum S

Part of the St Canice's Church complex built in 1864 by the Very Rev John Gorman (from Ballyragget and pastor of St Canice's from 1826). Unfortunately the cut stone walls are covered in pebble dash and the quoins with concrete.

St Canice's National School C

A fine stone gable facade with attractive cut stone surrounds to the door and two windows (with hood mouldings). The plaque above the door dates it to 1864. This facade should be preserved.

Nos 24 – 26 S

Two 2 storey and one 3 storey house which complete the terrace on this side of the street.

No 24 with its limestone sills, is blocked up as is all too common along this historic street.

No 30 S

A visually important building which closes this portion of Dean Street when approached from the west. An unusual hipped gable wall with rusticated 'keystones' topped by a pleasant roofscape.

Nos 31 – 38 S

Nos 37 and 38 have been deroofed and blocked up: Nos 34 and 35 have been removed altogether. This dereliction is unfortunate since the scale of the street here has an intimacy which makes the discovery of Friar's Bridge Street and the parting and curving of Dean Street all the more pleasant. No 32 is a nice house with a double window in the ground floor and rusticated 'keystones' throughout.

Stone Wall H

This wall has the remains of 3 stone window surrounds and 2 round arched stone doorways. On the outside gable wall of No 42 is a Tudor Fireplace 'hanging' on the wall. These remains appear to be part of a 16th century house which was at a slightly lower level than the existing street.

Nos 42 – 44 S

A very old terrace, with some old windows with glazing bars, which deserves restoration. An interesting fanlight above the door of No 42. The ground floor windows of No 44 are protected by wrought iron railings.

A plaque of the Shee Family on the wall of this terrace, now in Rothe House, indicated the possible site of the Archdekin House.

North Side: No 1 S

Tower House. A visually important building as it closes both St Canice's Place and Irishtown. A 3 storey building of excellent proportions. The upper floor windows retain glazing bars but the ground floor has been modernised unsympathetically to the detriment not of the building itself but Irishtown as a whole and the aspect of St Canice's.

Nos 2 – 10 S

This group of buildings has been mutilated. Nos 8 and 9 are missing; No 7 is unaltered and indicates the former appearance of Shanahan Furniture.

No 10, a 3 storey 6 bay house, stands on the corner of Coach Lane and therefore is visually important. A plaque, dated 1704, on

Former St Canice's School EOD

the South Wall bears the name George Gaffney. The window and door surrounds, with quatrefoil decorations in the stops are similar to No 19A.

Minogues

This area has been badly handled in view of its proximity to the St Canice's complex. The concrete and pebble dash walls with illuminated signs compare unfavourably with the adjacent stone walls. The planting of semi-mature deciduous trees on the waste area would be an improvement.

Nos 14 – 19A

Some of these 2 storey houses, viz 14 and 16, are blocked up but they maintain the street line. No 16 closes the view up Friars Bridge Street; No 17 bears the cast iron street sign 'Dean Street'.

No 19A is an attractive house with moulded surrounds to the door and windows. The stops to the door and ground floor window surrounds contain quatrefoil decoration, as does No 10.

St Canice's R.C. Church MQ

No 32 Dean St GT

BUTTS GREEN

The Butts Green is probably the oldest part of Kilkenny. It is referred to in the annals as 'the middle of Kilkenny'. It receives its name from the fact that the citizens practised archery at 'Butts' on the green.

South Side

This side includes a farm house, hay barn and cow shed — a fine example of 'rus in urbe'. No 28 is a fine old stone building which is now roofless and shored up and which no doubt will be demolished — although the Green needs some distinguished buildings. No 29A is a 3 storey building with a shop on the ground floor.

East Side: Donegan

This shop in a visually important position, with a dwelling house attached, is one of the few traditional buildings in the area to be retained in a well maintained condition. To the south-east the new front to Kelly's Corner Bar lacks distinction.

Nos 5 and 6

Two 2 storey dwellings, with a shop in the ground floor of No 5, with rendered facades, brick surrounds to the doors and windows, and stone sills. This building has commendably retained a cheerful, warm, aspect. To its north are 4 small 'cabins' which detract greatly from this area where sensitive infill buildings are required.

Cross   H

This cross at the northern end has a stone plaque in its base inscribed 'Improved by Kilkenny Corporation. Michael Kennedy Mayor 1891'.

It was at one time possible to decipher the arms of the Shee family and the letters RS and MF on the cross. It is thought to be a votive cross erected by Margaret Fagan in memory of her husband Richard Shee who died in 1608. There are more colourful legends in connection with its erection described in Hogan's Kilkenny.

FRIAR'S BRIDGE STREET

Links Dean Street and the Black Abbey. A street with a distinct 'industrial' feel, but the widespread use of limestone as an expressed building material permits the buildings to be compatible in this ecclesiastical area. Three ingredients which add to the charm of any street are present — narrowing, curvature, and inclination.

East Side: Nos 1 — 2   S

Two houses with nice scale and character.

Warehouse   C

T. Dore & Sons. A fine warehouse well built in random rubble with elliptically arched windows with brick dressings. Two ground floor windows have been badly concreted up: nearby is a gas lamp bracket. High on the gable wall is a fine circular opening with a brick surround containing a cart wheel. A brick basket arched entrance is adjacent. Formerly a Malt store and owned by Dores for about a century.

Blackmill St EOD

Friar's Bridge S
The eastern parapet should be lowered to afford a view of the Breagagh river (and the Dipper which is often to be seen). Local residents still throw refuse into the river.

A portion of the Black Abbey Cloister can be seen from the bridge.

West Side: Warehouse C
A good example of an industrial building of the period built in random rubble with openings with brick dressings. An attractive view of the undulating facade on the sloping ground is had from the Bridge.

Friar's Residence C
Built in 1894. There are few domestic buildings of this period in Kilkenny. The quality of the snecked stone work is, surely, unsurpassed in the locality and a long established tradition of working stone is evident. The openings have chamfered ashlar dressings: the two-light windows in the building are, on the first floor, topped with Tudor arches.

BLACKMILL STREET

This attractive street curves upwards from the Waterbarrack to St Mary's Cathedral. The contrast in scale between the houses and the dominating mass of the Cathedral is visually exciting and no new building or reconstruction should be allowed to upset this.

North East Side: Nos 1 — 18 S
The descending curve of this terrace from the Cathedral is really attractive. Nos 10 and 11 have pleasant original windows — with small upper sashes on the first floor.

No 19 S
Campion's Public House. A 3 storey 5 bay building. A good facade with rusticated keystones to the window surrounds and fluted pilasters with consoles terminating the ground floor. The coloured brick in one of the ground floor windows is discordant.

South West Side: Nos 22 — 27 S
No 22 is a pretty little house with original windows and nice scale.

No 28
These prefabricated buildings mar several of Kilkenny's streets since they show no regard to the character, scale and building line of their neighbours.

Nos 29 — 37 S
Some of these houses have been commendably refurbished, particularly No 30. No 34 however has been modernised out of character. Nos 36 and 37 retain their glazing bars.

No 38 H
A plaque denotes the fact that James Stephens, the Fenian leader, lived at this site.

James Stephens, founder, organiser and chief of the Fenian Brotherhood was born in a house which formerly occupied this site in 1825. He was educated in St Kieran's College and later worked for the Railway Company. His revolutionary career started with the 1848 Rising. In 1865 he escaped from Richmond Gaol, a hue and cry was started for his apprehension offering a reward of £1,000, a copy of which may be seen in Rothe House. He fled to France but later returned to Ireland where he died in 1901. The plaque to honour his memory was unveiled on 26th November 1967 by Mrs Joan Clarke with due ceremony.

Nos 39 — 42 S
Semi-detached houses with brick bay windows in which the bricks have been accentuated with paint — a common Irish practice which has been praised by some visiting town planners. The cast iron railings in front of the houses testify that until recently Kilkenny had an iron foundry.

THE COACH ROAD & CHURCH LANE

An entry in the Chapter Book of St Canice's Cathedral dated 20th September 1689 notes: 'Ordered that a convenient coach-way be made forthwith from Dean Street in Irishtown to the south door of the said Cathedral for the convenience of the Duke of Ormonde's family and other persons of quality resorting to the said Church'.

A pleasant laneway which runs from the Coach Road around the perimeter of the Cathedral grounds. The lanes leading off the lane, Coach Road, Common Hall Lane, St Canice's Steps, greatly add to the atmosphere of the area as does the random rubble walling. The telegraph wires should be put underground.

The Deanery   C
A 3 storey building with a light Gibbsian doorcase atop a flight of steps. Built between 1755 and 1784 on the site of an older building — the Deans 'Manse'. In earlier times the Dean's memorial residence was in St Patrick's Parish which was the prebend, or parish, of the dean. This residence was on the site of St Joseph's Convent and the townland is still called Deansby.

Sexton's House   S
See St Canice's Steps for description. Outside this house is one stone bollard. A second was knocked down during re-surfacing of the lane in 1975 (now fortunately replaced); and until recently, a third was present. These three bollards were colloquially known as Heaven, Hell (the central one) and Purgatory.

St Canice's Cathedral   AH
See Section 1, page 28.

St Canice's Library   SH
See Section 1, page 30.

No 10 Loreto View 1971   EOD

The Bishop's Palace   CH
See Section 1, page 31. A large 3 storey 5 bay building with a Gibbs doorcase (named after the architect James Gibbs) of monumental proportions. A fine iron coach gate and matching wicket gate (made in Dublin) front the grounds.

Loreto Convent   S
This twin towered house with attractive row of dormer windows which is the nucleus of the present Loreto convent was in the eighteenth century the townhouse of Viscount Clifden and called St James Park House. In 1789 Lord Clifden died and the house was purchased by the R.C. Ecclesiastical Authorities for use as a Diocesan College. It was to become known as The Old Academy. Later the students moved to Maudlin Street Seminary and in 1817 the lay students returned to their first house — Burrell's Hall. In 1868 the Loreto nuns came here from Borris-in-Ossory to start a girls day and boarding school. A programme of expansion started and has continued ever since.

LORETO VIEW

Nos 8 — 10   S
These 2 storey houses act as a visual stop to Church Lane and this important group should be maintained. It is unfortunate that the most strategic house, No 10, lacks its glazing bars — unlike its neighbours.

Nos 5 — 7   S
These small single storey cottages have a charm and scale entirely suited to this confined area, the facades being enlivened by the small paned windows. Behind them is the site of Black Rath Castle.

This Castle, a very ancient building, now part of the Library, probably originated as a defence work for the Cathedral and may have become a bastion of the city wall later. It must have served at some time as a manse house for the Prebendary (or Canon) of Blackrath. The Chapter of Ossory consists of a Dean, Archdeacon, Chancellor, Precentor and Treasurer with seven Prebendaries namely: Aghoure (now Freshford), Blackrath (now Maddoxtown), Clonamery, Killamery, Kilmanagh, Mayne and Tiscoffin. Apart from Blackrath and Killamery there is no evidence that the other Canons had Manse houses near the Cathedral since they employed stipendaries to carry out their duty of singing the office in the Cathedral. These stipendaries formed the Vicar's Choral and probably lived in community in the Common Hall.

ST CANICE'S PLACE

Links Dean Street to Vicar Street.

North Side: Monaghan's Warehouse S

This building flanks Velvet Lane and with the Tower House, No 1 Dean Street, partially closes the view from Irishtown towards St Canice's. The textural qualities of the facade visually link the Tower House and the Cathedral in an interesting manner. An inscribed plaque on the east side of the building records the name of Jacobus Shee who was procurator in 1647. (A similar plaque is on the east side of the small entrance to the Cathedral grounds).

No 10

Has now been insensitively blocked up and the roof removed. It is vital that any development on this site is handled in a sensitive manner.

The adjacent garage is unsuited to this area and an Amenity Study by Bolton Street College of Technology Architectural Students prepared in 1970 recommended the building of a screening wall.

South Side

In former times the eastern end was the probable location of the Bull Inn. A carving of a bull and inscribed 'Bulls Inn' was present in 1926. An illustration can be seen in 'Kilkenny' by Sparks and Bligh (1926). The upper floors of Walsh's, with an interesting roofscape, is the best remaining feature of the street.

No 27 Vicar St   EOD

VELVET LANE & ST CANICE'S STEPS

Velvet Lane runs from St Canice's Place to St Canice's Steps. The steps (of limestone and 26 in number) were erected in 1614 and they derive much of their character from their enclosure by the buildings in Velvet Lane. Set into the centre of the arch at the head of the steps is an inscribed stone with similar Latin inscriptions on the south and north sides recording the building of the steps by Robert Wale (Wall) Procurator of the Cathedral in 1614. The pavement on the east side of the Lane contains limestone flags (amongst the last in the City) which paved Kilkenny until well into the present century. There is an urgent need to attend to the buildings on the side of the lane and if replaced the new buildings should retain the existing building line and scale.

Sexton's House   S

At the top on the north west corner of the steps. Formerly the Procurator's House. Inserted in the gable is a splendid escutcheon bearing the arms of Edward VI emblazoned in deep relief with the inscription 'Edwarde Gra. Rexanglie Francie et Hibernie VI'. This stone must be dated between 1547 and 1553 and may represent public recognition of the King as head of the church instead of the Pope. Other sculptural stones on this gable include a very fine Archangel Michael.

Velvet Lane from Steps   BF

The Sexton's House   GT

VICAR STREET

Rises from St Canice's Place and runs to Troy's Gate. The dignitaries of St Canice's lived along this street, hence the name Vicar Street.

West Side: Nos 23 — 25   S

Nos 24 and 25 flank Common Hall Lane, another of the narrow entrances to the St Canice's complex.

No 24, a 2 storey 2 bay building built in 1905, features vermiculated rustication on the quoins and keystones. All the openings are topped with segmental arches. The ground floor has a two-light window.

No 26. An insensitive infill.

No 27   C

A very old building which is contemporary with the stables of the Bishop's Palace next door. It was formerly the workshop of John Crennan, Painter and Decorator, and the old facia bore his name in Irish. The openings, which contained 18th century sashes, were insensitively blocked up in 1975.

East Side: Nos 4 — 15   S

This row of old houses of different heights forms a very nice varied terrace to No 11, and the rhythm is continued in the upper storeys as far as No 15.

No 16

The former house of the Vicars Chorale, a building dating from the 16th century, though its foundation is attributed to Bishop Geoffry St Leger (1260-1287), has been replaced by a building totally out of keeping with the surroundings. This building also breaks the street line. It is possible to bring commerce and inject life into a street, which this development unquestionably does, without destroying its character and continuity in this way.

Troy's Gate MQ

Nos 17 — 19   S

A 2 storey group. No 17 has a hood moulding over the ground floor window showing it to be an old building with, originally, a lower street level. Tudor rear windows.

No 18 has a modernised ground floor but the upper storeys remain attractive with their stucco work and dentils. No 19 has interesting quoins and two double windows.

Nos 20 — 22   S

These 2 storey buildings were built by Nicholas Shortall in the 1860s and are visually important as a closure to St Canice's Place. The TV aerials are visually intrusive and spoil the skyline here as elsewhere. Formerly No 22 was possibly the Manse of the Prebendary of Tiscoffin.

COMMON HALL LANE

This lane leads in a most attractive wayward manner from the St Canice's Close to Vicar Street, and in particular passes the site of the Common Hall of the Vicar's Choral — of whom 8 lived in a community. Alongside the bend in the lane are two pleasant cottages, one in disrepair, which should be maintained.

TROY'S GATE

There is no longer any trace of the former Gate which stood here, but a small section of the old wall remains close by. Drysdale's Lane (named after the Chancellor of the Cathedral in 1688) at Troy's Gate, formerly a public laneway leading to the Cathedral, is now incorporated in the Bishop's Garden.

Troy's Gate Bar   C

A fine 3 storey 5 bay public house, well sited, with a strong late Victorian facade, which acts as a visual stop to Green Street. This building should be retained.

The landscaping of the open spaces either side of the junction with semi-mature indigenous deciduous trees and the relocation of the street furniture would make a significant contribution to the townscape. This area has potential but at present is as inhuman as the motor car for which the adjacent buildings were presumably sacrificed.

GREEN STREET

Runs from Troy's Gate to Green's Bridge. Formerly an attractive street, the re-routing of the road has resulted in an insensitive south side. However, much of the north side is well maintained and the planting of the 'Green' with indigenous trees and the landscaping of the river bank would create a charming cul-de-sac. Some trees were planted in 1975 and further work could create a charming, even picturesque, residential area.

North Side: Corner — No 29

An uninteresting part of the street where the most noticeable features are the break in the legend 'Mulhalls Flour and Corn Store' caused by an opening for a first floor door; and the Tudor type chimney on the gable of the adjoining premises. With painting the appearance of the Store, with its many openings of different sizes, could be improved (c.f. Molloy's store, St Kieran Street).

No 28 — 23   S

The future of this group seems certain as the result of recent re-roofing. The painting of some of the facades accentuates the individual elements in the group.

Nos 22 — 20

These two houses are unoccupied but hopefully they will be repaired and occupied — thus maintaining the unity of the street.

Shop front, Green St   EOD

Nos 19 — 17   S

A good group of houses with the unused shop indicating to the onlooker the absence of a community that once supported it. Three little features add to the area: the 'Green Street' plaque set on a quoin, the limestone kerb stones, and the neat bush growing around the telegraph pole.

Green's Bridge   C

Designed by G. Smith and built by Colles to replace one which was swept away in the great flood of 1764. Smith also designed John's Bridge at the smae time and the cost of building these two bridges in 1765 was £5,407. It is a six arched Palladian style limestone bridge of fine proportions, which was widened during the closure of John's Bridge in 1969. This alteration, which ruins it from the north side, was intended to be a temporary measure and the stones of the wall were accordingly numbered when removed. Surely the wall could be replaced and an elegant footbridge cantilevered from the stone structure. The parapets were added to the Bridge in 1835.

JOHN'S QUAY

Runs from John's Bridge northwards on the east bank of the River Nore. The buildings along John's Quay form an attractive group which is unsurpassed in Kilkenny. Georgian, Victorian and Edwardian architecture exhibiting good proportions and some fine craftsmanship all in pleasant surroundings. Three discordant notes are struck by the pollarded trees, the recent isolation of the Library, and the savage treatment to the windows in the Home Rule Club.

No 2   S

An early Georgian 3 storey 4 bay detached house which formerly had a slate hung gable, of which traces remain. The top floor has 4 small windows with 3 pane sashes; all the other windows have modern single pane sashes. A plain fanlighted doorcase with three simple indented pateras and some fluting on the lintel — charming vernacular architecture.

No 3   C

Home Rule Club. An excellent 3 storey 5 bay detached Georgian building with a plastered facade. The ground floor windows, most disastrously, have been nearly blocked up: elsewhere millions of windows were sensitively blocked up by our forebears to evade the window tax. Five windows, with 6 pane sashes on the 2 floors above. Along the top of the facade is a cornice. The excellent doorcase (surely by the same mason as 88, 89 John Street and 12, 13 Kieran Street) has 2 engaged Tuscan columns; the entablature has a central oval patera flanked by fluting and round pateras; the surround to the excellent fanlight has an oval patera flanked by fluting and round pateras.

This building, formerly the Nore View School, was built some time before 1840 as a Feinaiglian School following the system of memory training invented by Dr Gregory von Feinaigle who flourished in Dublin from 1811 to 1819. Its headmaster Dr James St John died in 1873 when presumably the school closed.

No 4   S

An attractive detached 2 storey Georgian house topped with cornice and low parapet with high chimneys in character. The modest doorcase has jambs with blocks of stone, quoinwise, punctuating the jamb, which has a narrow raised band as does the elliptical fanlight — all in well figured limestone. The ground floor has 2 two-light windows with six pane sashes: the first floor has 2 two-light and a single window with six pane sashes.

Nos 5 and 6   C

A 3 storey 4 bay Georgain detached building with an excellent portico to the 2 entrance doors flanked by railings with cast iron spear head tops. The pedimented portico with three pilasters, with a band of fluting on each, is probably the work of the Colles family. Above the cornice is a small stepped parapet — possibly Kilkenny Egyptian Revival. The ground floor has a three-light window each side of the portico; the first floor has 4 two-light windows with 4 pane sashes; the second floor has 4 windows with 2 pane sashes.

This building is commonly known as Priors Orchard as it is sited in the former orchard of St John's Priory.

Carnegie Library   S

This pleasant classical style building was erected in 1910, the site having been given by Ellen, Countess of Desart. Through the years it has suffered much from the flooding of the Nore. The facade has a semi-

John's Quay GD

circular portico supported by 2 Tuscan columns over 4 steps. The portico, with a small tower over, is flanked by 2 gables, each containing a large round headed window. Railings fronted the library until recently when a car park was made. The railings provided a visual link between the library and the neighbouring buildings which is now sadly lacking.

Nos 7 and 8   C

A 2 storey semi-detached building with a rendered facade fronted by a small garden, low wall and railings. The facade is finished with brick 'quoins' and the openings are dressed with brick. A cast iron plaque on No 7 reads 'Founded 1888 by the Corporation. Megan Mayor 1887 — 1888'.

Nos 9 — 17   C

A 2 storey terrace identical to Nos 7 and 8. These house are simple and attractive with excellent proportions. When bathed in sunlight the terrace has a warm, friendly air. Their unity should be conserved and merits a preservation order.

The Carnegie Library EOD

JOHN STREET LOWER

Runs from John's Bridge to the East. This part of Kilkenny east of John's Bridge is popularly known as 'The Continent'.

North Side: No 1 S
Smyths. 3 bay 3 storey (over basement) John Street facade with four steps up to a Gibbsian doorcase. Glazing bars to all windows. The charming nineteenth century shopfront (with a second entrance to the cosy interior from the John's Quay facade) with its robust signwriting was replaced in 1975 by a 'Neo-Georgian' doorcase.

The hipped roofs of this building and that of No 88 and 89 when viewed from the Bridge make a harmonious pair and, with the inclination and curvature of the street, invite exploration. Note the scale of the buildings on the south side when viewed from this point.

No 2 S
A residential building with a cast iron balcony to the first floor.

No 3 S
No 3 has 2 light windows (with 6 pane sashes) with good architraves to all 3 storeys. The diminutive double doorway, contrasting in scale to the windows makes this a lively facade.

No 5
Heffernan, features an early twentieth century shop front the facia of which records in varied wooden lettering the proprietor's name and occupation (Woodworker) in an imaginative manner. Two pilasters containing carved Art Nouveau decoration, remain. A wrought iron bracket, formerly carrying a sign, projects from the facade.

No 10 S
A 2 storey 3 bay building with shopfront the window of which announces in a dignified manner, gold Roman lettering on black ground, 'Finnegan Turf Accountant'.

Nos 11 and 12 S
No 12, J. O'Reilly. A well maintained shopfront with 3 pilasters. The facia with excellent signwriting is terminated with elaborately carved consoles with acanthus leaf decoration.

Nos 13 and 14 S
No 14, The Sports Centre. With its considerately painted facade (of blue with the ground floor pilasters, architraves to the first and second floor windows, sashes with glazing bars, and stucco quoins picked out in white) is of more interest than No 13.

No 15
The Wine Centre. A 3 storey 3 bay building with an out-of-character ground floor with projecting illuminated box facia and facing of random stone, marble and mosaic tiles. Above, the windows have shouldered architraves.

No 16 C
The Garden Centre. A 5 bay residential building of 3 storeys in which the ground floor was recently converted for commercial use with more care and consideration than any other building in Kilkenny (except the Kilkenny Design Workshops which was an equestrian residence). The ground floor openings have been removed and replaced by arches of a similar size to the westernmost arch which is original. The shopfront is recessed behind the piers permitting goods to be displayed in the open. Surely a modern successor to the old and almost extinct practice of displaying goods on the pavement, hanging from the facade and the stays of projecting awnings.

The origins of this building form stretch back four centuries to the arcaded facade of Rothe House, The Langton House, etc.

The windows above all have architraves with 6 pane sashes to the first floor and 3 pane sashes to the second floor.

The facade is topped by a cyma recta cornice returned to the brick gable. The gutter is carried clear on long arm brackets which echo the shape of the cornice.

The building is well maintained and with No 16 next door, makes the most interesting streetscape pairing in Kilkenny. Here there is a contrast in scale, character and age — all three qualities being obvious. Nos 10 and 11 High Street, another fine pairing, only contrast in character.

No 17 C
McCormack. A 3 storey building of one bay with original sash windows. The maroon Georgian ground floor shopfront has 3 hollow pilasters double door with simple Adamesque fanlight, facia with good but faded signwriting, and filleted ovolo cornice. The building has a charm of the highest order and with the recent alterations to No 9, Irishtown it is currently the oldest, most intact shopfront in Kilkenny. Yet a generation ago it would have been considered one of the most insignificant facades. The view to this facade and that of the Garden Centre fronted by the chesnut tree from Kilkenny College is one of the most pleasant in the town.

No 18
No 18, structurally the same building as No 17, has none of its charm.

Nos 19 — 21 S
A 2 storey building each of 2 bays with dormer windows to No 20.

Under the road beside No 19 is the course of a mill race which left the Nore at Noremount, Greenshill, and returned at the end of Maudlin Street where some remains of a mediaeval mill can be seen.

No 19 has a random rubble gable with brick dressings to the openings. The facade has 2 illuminated projecting signs.

No 21 has been modernised to such an extent that none of the original external features remain on any floor. The gable faces up John Street and is an important visual stop. Up Barrack Lane beside this building is a fresh looking manhole cover from the former DeLoughrey Foundry which exhibits neat raised Roman lettering.

Terminating Barrack Lane is a cut-stone gateway giving access to St John's Priory and the Evans Poor House. There is a small doorway on the right which can be used when the large gate is closed. For St John's Priory see page 32.

Evans' Poor House   C

The history of this part of the monastery grounds after the suppression in 1540 is obscure. The Monastery property passed to the Corporation of Kilkenny and it is known that at some stage the nave was thrown down in order to build a barracks. The lane leading from John's Street to the Church gateway, west of the present graveyard is still known as Barrack Lane.

It appears that the barracks was no longer in use as a barracks in 1818, possibly having been replaced by the present barracks on the Castlecomer Road. The site near St John's Priory was acquired by the Evans Trust, set up under the will of Joseph Evans of Belevan who died in 1818, and the present building was erected or converted as an almshouse. About the same time the Lady Chapel of the monastery was re-roofed and restored as a Protestant Church and

Evans' Poor House   MQ

Nos 5 to 17 John St   GD

John's Abbey 1861   KC, JD

P. M. Egan cites Mr Robertson as the architect who supervised this restoration. Roberston may have also designed the almshouse.

A 2 storey building with skirting plinth in coursed rubble subsequently rendered, which has a pleasing intimate scale despite its size.

Removal of the dull rendering, repointing, replacement of the casements with sash windows, and landscaping of the grounds (with its good views) would make this an exciting building with its unusual layout, doorcases, good proportions and textural qualities.

South Side: Nos 62 and 63   S

Lawlors, formerly the Crystal Bar and Corcorans. A visually important building standing on the corner of Maudlin Street. A well maintained 2 storey building with applied quoins and moulded window surrounds, with glazing bars to the first floor windows. The facade is marred by a large illuminated projecting sign.

Nos 64 and 65   S

Two 3 storey buildings. The ground floor of No 64 has been modernised in the usual manner, but the upper windows of it and No 65, wih their glazing bars, are pleasant.

McGrath (John Street Post Office) has an ordinary nineteenth century ground floor shopfront with dentils to the cornice adding a little dash.

Nos 66 — 70   S

The upper floors of these 3 storey buildings maintain, in general, the character of the street with most of the glazing bars remaining.

No 67, Lewis, is the most attractive in this respect and the ground floor, with its petrol pumps, gives the building an Irish-provincial-town atmosphere.

Two ground floors lack this Irish character, namely Roma Cafe (with its imitation marble, aluminium, and facia which destroys the proportions of the first floor windows) and No 68, Hogan, (with its projecting facia box and full width window).

Nos 69 and 70, Edward Langton. The facade with sensitive painting, signwriting and the use of a traditional projecting sign had been recently transformed from anonymity to one of charm and personality. An object lesson to all traders.

No 71   S

An imposing house, with chamfered stone quoins and cornice, which appears to be eighteenth century, though it is probably earlier. The windows no longer have glazing bars. The west gable is of random rubble with brick in the apex: the east gable is weatherslated. The door has a Gibbsian surround (similar to Nos 42 & 43 Parliament Street) with a strange, distracting lozenge shape in the fanlight. Until around 1930 this building was a police barracks. Painting of the rendering would enliven the facade.

Kilkenny College   AH

Kilkenny College on the left bank of the river, is best seen from the Castle gardens or the Canal Walk where the view of the school and its lawns and playgrounds is both imposing and impressive.

The College was founded in 1667 by James, 1st Duke of Ormonde (an earlier Ormonde school near St Canice's Cathedral was by then defunct). In his capacity as Viceroy he granted it a Charter in 1684, this date being inscribed on the gate. The school had a frontage on John Street and was a building on the style of Rothe House with an imposing double stepped entrance of which only the hood mouldings of the doorways remain where the gateway now stands. A painting of this school was to be seen formerly in Kilkenny Castle.

In 1782 the old school was taken down and the present structure erected, a 7 bay Georgian building 8 bays deep. The decorated doorway is, probably, the most beautiful one in Kilkenny. It is flanked by paired pilasters with sidelights; the huge full width fanlight has a surround with heavy cavetto moulding. The survival of the original glazing in a school is noteworthy.

Its many famous past pupils include Jonathan Swift, George Berkeley, William Congreve, George Farquaher (probably) and the brothers John and Michael Banim who left a description of the old school in a novel 'The Fetches'.

A short lived University of St Canice was established here by James II in February 1690, but it closed in July of the same year after the Battle of the Boyne.

Nos 73 — 75   S

Late Victorian 2 storey terrace houses. Segmental arches to the door, ground floor double windows, and first floor single windows.

Rendered facade with alternate red and white brick dressings to the openings. The dressings to No 75 are painted grey. Special bricks form a bracketed eaves cornice.

Nos 76 and 77

The Furniture Centre. A 2 storey 4 bay building with heavy cornice and shaped gutter, the ground floor of which has been modernised out of character.

Nos 78 — 81

This 3 storey group bears the Fitzgerald-Shee coat of arms. This family was evicted during the Cromwellian era in the mid-seventeenth century. There are signs of an ancient building to the rear with an old fireplace and corbel stones set in a wall.

Nos 79 and 80 have cornices on consoles to first floor windows.

Kilkenny College MQ

The Bridge House EOD

Ceiling, Bridge House MF

No 81, The Bridge Bar. The bottom edge of the timber facia has a nailhead pattern. This pattern can be seen on the consoles to the cornices, and also on the side door of No 88.

Nos 83 and 84
A 3 storey building. No 83, Dowling has a black shopfront with chromed letters, and the windows above have glazing bars in contrast to No 84.

No 84, O Farrell, retains an old shopfront but the windows above lack glazing bars.

No 86 S
J. Casey. A 3 storey building with an arched coach entrance beside. The first and second floor windows are, unusually, the same size and retain their glazing bars. The upper floors are well proportioned.

No 87 S
Hotel Carmel. A 3 storey building with the gutter supported on paired brackets with a course of bricks laid in echelon below.

Nos 88 and 89 B
The Bridge House. A fine 3 storey building with a Georgian facade and seven steps, flanked by railings, up to an excellent double doorcase. Two Tuscan engaged columns support an entablature with pateras and a fluted frieze: a breakforward is over the columns. There is a bow, with 3 windows per floor, to the front of No 89 (c.f. rear of Butler House, Patrick Street) and all windows have 6 pane sashes. Beside the building is a groin vaulted entrance to the rear cobbled courtyard and outbuildings. The rear of the building shows that the house was originally Tudor with mullions, doors, etc, visible. The main reception rooms with stucco adornments and mantelpieces are probably the finest rooms in Kilkenny. The house once had a dovecote. By virtue of its architecture and position by the river and closing, or partially closing the view, from three directions this building must be regarded as one of the finest in Kilkenny.

Dr Butler (tomb in St Mary's) was host here to Maria Edgeworth. Members of the National Army took up defensive positions here during the Civil War and bullet holes may be observed around one of the windows. See also pages 39 and 40.

John's Bridge C
Built in 1910 the Bridge was the longest single span ferro-concrete bridge in the British Isles and considered a great engineering feat. The engineer in charge was Alexander Burden. In 1969/70 it underwent a complete overhaul and was strengthened. The Corporation wisely replaced the attractive gas lamp holders which adorned the previous bridge. At the S.W. extremity are two incised stone plaques. The upper, circular, reads 'The Right Honourable Earl of Desart 1810'. The lower, rectangular, reads, 'The above was taken from the old and placed on the new St John's Bridge. Designed in the mayoralty of The Hon Otway Cuffe Mayor of Kilkenny 1907-1908. Grandson of the above named Earl of Desart'.

At the N.W. extremity is a stone plaque reading '1910 St John's Bridge. Rebuilt by the Corporation and Co Council of Kilkenny. Ald Michael L. Potter JP Mayor 1908-1910'.

MAUDLIN STREET

This narrow winding street runs from John Street to the Dublin Road through what was originally a strongly fortified bawn which protected the grain and other agricultural stores of the Kilkenny Castle. From early times this street was the main thoroughfare carrying all the traffic from the east, until the main Dublin Road was established around 1820. It has retained much of its character despite unsympathetic development, e.g. prefabricated houses and industrial premises. Any new buildings should maintain the present scale and building lines. The river and castle can be viewed in places and those visual links are important. To the west of the street are some slight remains of an early Butter Mill and the water course which powered it. (It ran parallel to the Nore from Noremount, north of Green's Bridge, passed under John's Street and rejoined the river at the eastern end of Maudlin Street. It was filled in around 1930.)

Apart from Nos 9 — 12 (modern single storey buildings which lack character) the houses on Maudlin Street have a theme which runs down much of the street, namely, paired doors sometimes with paired windows above. Some of the houses are badly neglected, presumably because the local authority wants to widen the street. However, this is not necessary as its width is perfectly adequate for one way traffic. The existing houses should be repaired, which is considerably cheaper than demolishing and rebuilding. The occasional house could be removed to provide off-the-street parking for neighbouring residents.

At the bottom of many of the gardens on the west side is an overgrown lane. This might be cleared to give residents an extension of the riverside Lacken Walk through to John Street via Kilkenny College.

Magdalen Castle AH

A 25m high castle with a pronounced base batter. One of three castles or Tower Houses built by William the Earl Marshall protecting an agricultural enclosure of the Castle. From the fourteenth to the sixteenth century this close was used as a leper settlement, thus giving the castle and street the name of Magdalen. Later a gate attached to the Castle served as the eastern gate of the extended city of Kilkenny. Within the close there was a church dating from early times and the graveyard remains. Successive churches were dedicated to St Stephen, St Mary Magdalen and St John. The remains of the latter being removed around 1960.

Nos 34 and 35

Numbers 34 and 35 at the entrance to the graveyard were formerly a single house, used by the Catholic clergy of St John's Parish, and during the proscribed period as a Catholic Bishop's residence. Dr Thomas de Burgo, Bishop of Ossory 1759-76, lived here. His history of the Irish Dominican Order (in Latin) is well known.

At the corner of No 34 next to the graveyard entrance is a milestone recording the distance from Dublin as 57 Irish miles. This stone dates from the eighteenth century when Maudlin Street was the only entrance to Kilkenny from the north-east.

Nursery House C

Beside No 88 a passageway leads to Fitz-Gerald's charming nursery at the bottom of which solidly stands a fine three storey house with a hipped slated roof which formerly was probably part of a mill.

Bastion HS

Beside No 89 at some stage before its dissolution the Priory of St John the Evangelist was enclosed by walls with outer and inner gates. This edifice is the remains of one of the bastions of the outer gate.

Magdalen Castle EOD

The Bastion EOD

MICHAEL STREET

Michael Street runs from the site of St Michael's gate of the Priory of St John northwards parallel to the river to join Green's Bridge Street. It is also called Abbey View Terrace (southern end) and St Malla's Terrace (northern end).

Nos 53 — 46, 45 — 31, 30 — 22   S

Three 2 storey terraces which formerly had a good view to the west over the town. This view is now greatly obstructed by recent buildings. To the south of No 53 is a new factory-built bungalow which is out of character.

From No 31 an excellent view of much of the town can be had. The southern portion of this view is bounded by the Castle and St Mary's Cathedral on the horizon. Between can be seen much interesting roofscape, random rubble to the rear of the High Street buildings, and the facades of 6 and 7 Parliament Street adding specks of colour. The northern quadrant from St Mary's to Green's Bridge is dominated by two huge buildings which by chance have a gap between them permitting Abbey View Terrace inhabitants a view of part of St Francis Abbey and St Canice's Cathedral.

Those who wish to absorb the past of this fine city and speculate on its future, stand here and look awhile.

Nos 20 — 10

Another 2 storey terrace which has a stone plaque on No 12 saying 'Erected under the Corporation Building Scheme. John Magennis Mayor of Kilkenny 1914-1915 and 1916'. These plaques which were quite common around the turn of the century add interest to the buildings they adorn, inform the passer-by, provide patronage to stone cutters, and provide evidence of the work of the incumbent mayor. The practice should be revived.

Francis McManus was born in No 20. See page 42.

Nos 11, 12 and 13 retain their original windows with glazing bars.

View from Michael St GD

JOHN STREET UPPER

John Street Upper was an unimportant laneway until the building of the Dublin Road about 1820. It then became a main entry to the town, increasing in importance when the railway terminus was built at its eastern end.

North Side: Nos 21 — 26

A 2 storey terrace in which No 21, Brett, has been unsympathetically modernised with a projecting canopy over the ground floor windows: this is unfortunate as it is situated on the corner of Michael Street in a visually important position.

Nos 24 and 25, Mascot Stores and Fitzpatrick are charming little shops with the ground floor pilasters and woodwork painted in imitation grain and enhanced by good signwriting. 'Home Made Confectionery Fresh Daily' on a panel on the former and 'General Drapery' on the latter. Michael Banim's Sports Shop occupied one or other of these little shops. It had an Irish half-door over which the author was often found leaning to greet the passers-by.

Nos 26 and 27

An excellent example of modern infill totally out of character with its neighbours.

Nos 28 — 31

Two 2 storey buildings. The shopfronts of 28 and 29, Norwood and G. Murphy, are similar in scale to Nos 24 and 25. Glazing bars are retained in the first floor windows of No 30.

Nos 32 and 33

Railway Hotel. A 3 storey 5 bay building with a heavily pebbledashed facade marred by a gaudy projecting sign. Inside the front entrance are two fine etched glass doors containing the words 'Hotel' and 'Bar' in the overall design.

The Railway Station 1861 KC

Nos 34 and 35

No 34 has been modernised in an unsympathetic manner.

No 35, O'Connell (City Lime Works) was formerly a most important premises as lime was burnt in a kiln to the rear until 1950 and sold to farmers as far away as Ullard (20 miles). Sadly the kiln has just been demolished.

No 36   S

P. Brady. A well maintained 2 storey building with stucco quoins with moulded surrounds and keystones to the two first floor windows. The ground floor shopfront has 4 fluted pilasters of which the outer pair have consoles terminating the facia and supporting its cornice.

Nos 37 and 38   S

A pair of 2 storey dwelling with a rendered facade with brick surrounds to the windows and doors. A stone plaque reads 'Founded by the Corporation, Michael Kennedy Mayor 1891'.

O'Gorman   S

A building in an important position defining the entrance to John's Green and seen from many angles.

South Side: Lawlors Bar   S

An excellently maintained 2 storey bar which faces the Dublin Road and, extensively, John Street Upper. It is located in one of the most important visual positions in Kilkenny.

Gray, Electrician

Modern infill which is out of character with its surroundings on account of its projecting canopy, strong horizontal emphasis, and flat roof which conflicts strongly with its neighbours.

Nos 54 — 60   S

These buildings are not noteworthy but they do have a scale which is in character with the size of the street and contrasts favourably with, for example, the Kilkenny Motor Company. The value of these buildings derives from their grouping, physical size and scale of business. Any out-of-character modernisation to any of the elements would upset the entire group. The character of this side of the street seems to be in the balance.

No 59 has a small attractive and unusual iron window railing. No 60, Muldowney and Quinn, is well maintained and decoration has made the most of its modest features to the benefit of the street.

DUBLIN ROAD

Built around 1820 to join the turn-pike road from Carlow with Upper John Street.

Off the Dublin Road is O'Loughlin Road, formerly Williams Lane, an old entrance to Kilkenny which joined the Carlow Road in Maudlin Street. Now named for the O'Loughlin family who built St John's Catholic Church.

North East Side: Railway Station

The Waterford and Kilkenny Railway Co was authorised in 1845 to establish a railway between the two towns. The first section to Thomastown was built by Messrs Wright & O'Toole and opened on 11th May, 1848. The Board Minutes for 5th August 1846 report that Captain Moorsom, the Engineer, presented a 'Design for a terminus station at Kilkenny which was generally approved of'. On 12th May 1847 Moorsom reported that a modified plan for the station had been made by Sancton Wood (architect to the G.S. & W.R. and I.S.E.R. and designer of Heuston Station) to permit it to take the additional traffic of the proposed Kilkenny-Carlow track (operated by the I.S.E.R.) which opened on 14th November, 1850.

The first plan for the station was estimated at £14,000 but when finished in late 1847 cost £31,471. The station at that time, with a happy combination of brick with Kilkenny limestone and tall Georgian windows was pleasant with an attractive northern facade which included the main entrance. However, by 1868 the line had been extended through this facade to Maryborough and Mountmellick.

The station was renamed in 1966 after Thomas MacDonagh, the 1916 leader, who once lived in Kilkenny.

Wind Gap Cottage TB

Wind Gap Cottage HS

This Georgian-Gothic house at the top of the hill was the home of John Banim from 1835 until his death in 1842. See page 42.

South West Side

The view south west as one enters Kilkenny is potentially the most attractive first glimpses any town could desire. However, the view is obscured by an ugly plastered wall and an undisciplined growth of scrub which threaten to choke the many fine trees which were planted in more enlightened times.

St John's Hall

This manse-like building was erected on a totally unsuitable site as a Catholic boys school in 1829. It was converted to a Parochial Hall around 1950. Its roof line is out of keeping with the terrace of houses which flows gently down from it and it blocks the view of Wind Gap Hill and the River.

St John's Graveyard

An old graveyard containing the graves of many of the oldest Kilkenny families including the historian Bishop Thomas de Burgo and writers John and Michael Banim, P. M. Egan and Robert Cane.

St John's Church

This church replaced an older one on the site of the graveyard. Built in 1903, the entire cost was borne by the O'Loughlin family of Sandford's Court. The site was presented to the parish by the 3rd Marquess of Ormonde. The spire, planned by architects William Hogan and William H. Byrne, was never erected. The spacious grounds are well planted with trees and shrubs.

JOHN'S GREEN

Prior to the establishment of the railway this area was a waste space outside the city. During the eighteenth century, it became the refuge of the dispossessed farming folk and other travelling people. They erected primitive dwellings, without plan, which became known as the Shower of Houses, and the last of which was removed around 1930. It was an area of poverty and distress. A gallows for miscreants functioned in John's Green (formerly known as Gallows Green).

Governor's House   S

Between John's Green and Upper John Street is the house which used to be the residence of the Governor of the Barracks. A 2 storey 4 bay building with stone chamfered quoins and a Gibbsian surround to the door topped by a slightly pointed fanlight. The windows have 6 pane sashes.

BARRACK STREET

Runs from John's Green under the disused railway bridge to the Castlecomer Road.

The Ormonde House   S

Properly known as the Hospital of Our Most Holy Lord and Saviour Jesus Christ, of the City of Kilkenny, and established by Walter Butler, 11th Earl of Ormonde. The 10th Earl (Black Tom) had willed that a hospital be built in a waste place near the old Tholsel of Kilkenny. In 1839, the 2nd Marquess of Ormonde moved the Alms House to its present site. The Ormonde House, No 5 High Street, was erected on the original site. The 'Master' of the Alms House is usually the Ormonde agent and the Butler family continue to take an interest in the home which has accommodation for seven inmates.

WOLFE TONE STREET

Runs from John's Green to the north. On the east side of the street is a shoe factory which was built around 1934.

Nos 4 — 8   S

A single storey terrace with stone sills and a series of bricks acting as brackets to the moulded gutter. A plaque states that the terrace was 'Founded by the Corporation, Alderman David Fenton Mayor 1890'. Nos 4, 6 and 7 have their original glazing bars.

Nos 9 — 33   S

A single storey terrace with dormer windows (with bargeboards) above, stone sills and brick chimneys. No 16 has the original 2 pane sash windows.
Opposite Nos 9 — 22 is a 2.5 high wall of coursed rubble in good condition.

Nos 34 — 42, 43 — 46   S

Two single storey terraces with rendered facades with brick surrounds to the doors and windows — which have stone sills. The bricks are painted and these houses look neat and warm. No 39 retains 4 pane sashes.

CASTLECOMER ROAD

Military Barracks

Officially named James Stephen Barracks in commemoration of the Fenian leader.

It was built during the period 1800 — 1803 to a design standard to the British Board of Works by the Kilkenny contractor James Switzir. Other identical barracks are the McCann Barracks, Templemore, and the Columb Barracks, Mullingar.

HEBRON ROAD

Workhouse   C

Workhouses were built after the passing of the 1834 Poor Law Act until about 1845. The advent of the Famine necessitated further building which continued until 1853. All follow a similar plan designed by Wilkinson, an Office of Public Works architect.

A huge well constructed 3 storey snecked ashlar building. The central block of 17 bays is flanked to the west by two advanced gables with attic storey of one bay each and to the east by 3 similar advanced gables. All windows have lozenge glazing. The advanced gables feature three-light windows with relieving arches above. Above ridge height the chimneys are of brick with stone cornices. The ridge of the central block is terminated by a lantern at each end.

The building, presently used by an engineering firm, is gradually deteriorating with glazing and slates missing, etc. In other countries such buildings have been converted into regional folk museums. Its location by the railway line would suggest its possible use as a National Transport Museum.

In front of the Workshop is a separate building of snecked ashlar in the same Tudor style. A 2 storey 3 bay central block flanked by a slightly advanced shouldered gable. In the central block the tops of the first floor windows are at eaves level so are topped by a small shouldered gable: the ground floor Tudor door is flanked by 2 lights with a hood moulding linking the composition: all openings have heavily chamfered surrounds. The openings of the advanced gables are likewise chamfered and those on the first floor in addition have voussoirs. The first floor window in the east end wall has both voussoirs and a relieving arch. Brick chimneys top the building.

John's Green EOD

41 and 42 Wolfe Tone St EOD

The Ormonde Alms House EOD

Architectural Glossary

Advanced
An area of a building which is proud of the surrounding area. Shown above is an advanced bay.

Aedicule
The framing of a door or window with 2 columns, piers or pilasters supporting a gable, lintel or an entablature and pediment.

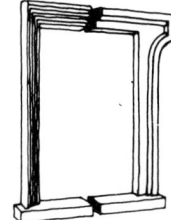

Architrave
The lowest member of an entablature (q.v.), also a moulding surrounding a window or door. Shown above, on the right, is a shouldered architrave.

Arris
A sharp edge produced by two meeting surfaces.

Art Nouveau
A flowing style of (in Ireland) about 1900 — 1914.

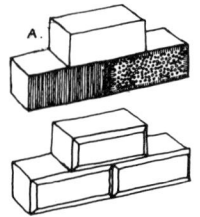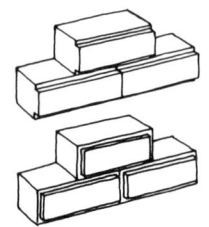

Ashlar
Regularly squared stonework. Chamfered: when the stones are separated by V-joints. Banded: when the horizontal joints are emphasised. Channelled: when the horizontal and vertical joints are emphasised. Stone finishes in illustration. A: smoothdressed; drag finished; pecked finish with dragged border.

Attic
The storey above the cornice (q.v.).

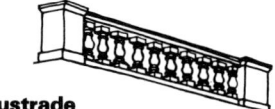

Balustrade
A series of short posts, or balusters, supporting a rail or coping (q.v.).

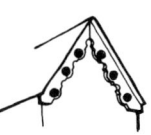

Barge-boards
Timber planks following the line of a gable where the roof overhangs the wall-face; sometimes decoratively carved or pierced.

Barrel-vault
A vault (q.v.) whether structural or simulated consisting of a semi-circular section.

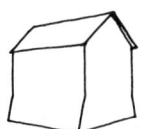

Base batter
An outward slope near the bottom of a wall.

Bay
A unit of design expressed by one window, horizontally considered (as opposed to 'storey' which is a vertical unit). A house five windows wide is said to be of five bays.

Block-and-Start
A common type of door and window surround in which the vertically placed stones alternate with horizontally set stones.

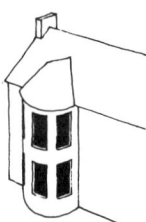

Bow
A curved projection from a building.

Bracket
A projection designed as a support.

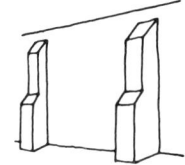

Buttress
A short length of wall at right-angles to the main wall, for the purpose of stiffening it against thrust. Often in diminishing projection in stages towards the top.

Capital
The decorative head of a column (q.v.) or pilaster (q.v.).

Cavetto
A concave moulding whose profile is usually a quarter circle.

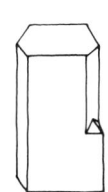

Chamfer
A diagonal surface produced by cutting off a corner, usually at 45°. Stopped chamfer: a chamfer not carried the length of the piece. Chamfered stone: see ashlar.

Chancel
The eastern part of a church, reserved for the choir, the monks or the clergy, as opposed to the nave (q.v.).

Churchwarden Glazing
Simple carpenters decorative tracery (q.v.). Usually of intersecting lines.

Classical
A style ultimately deriving from Greek and Roman architecture, but capable of great simplicity while remaining recognisable, characterised by square or round tops to the doors and windows, and usually symmetrical.

Column
The principal element in one of the classical orders (q.v.) consisting of a vertical shaft, standing on a base and supporting a capital.

Console
A scrolled bracket. Also a terminating feature to a facia on a shopfront.

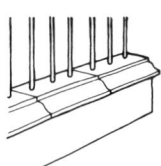

Coping
A protective capping to a wall to carry off water.

Corbel
A stone projecting from a wall and acting as a support to a beam or other feature, or to an oversailing course of masonry.

Corinthian
One of the three principal classical orders (q.v.) in which the capital is basket-shaped with acanthus-leaves curling out of it.

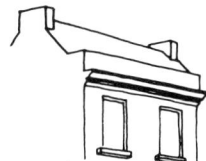

Cornice
The top part of an entablature (q.v.). Also any moulded projection which tops the part to which it is fixed, e.g. door window or wall. It may be surmounted by a balustrade (q.v.) or parapet, etc.

Course
A horizontal row of stones or bricks.

Crenellation
An up-and-down termination to a wall. The same as battlements.

Crest Tile
One of a series of ornamental ridge tiles.

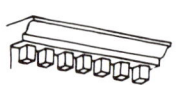

Dentil
One of a series of small cubical blocks set close together forming part of the ornamentation of some cornices (q.v.) and occasionally string-courses (q.v.).

Doric
One of the three principal classical orders (q.v.). In both Greek and Roman Doric the capital (q.v.) is surmounted by a plain shallow square block (called the abacus). A Greek Doric column has no base.

Dormer
A window occurring in the slope of the roof, giving light to an attic in the roof-space. A dormer has a little roof of its own.

Dressings
The stones, or sometimes the bricks, which are used to frame openings. Many buildings of random rubble (q.v.) have cut stone dressings. Also used to form string-courses, cornices, etc.

Eaves
The name given to the junction of wall and roof.

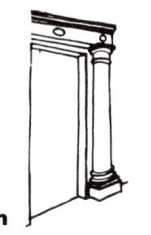

Engaged Column
A column (q.v.) which appears to be partly embedded in the wall behind it.

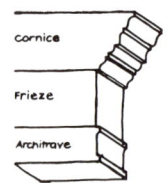

Entablature
The system of architrave (bottom), frieze (middle) and cornice (top) which sits on top of the column in the classical order.

Fanlight
The window, usually semi-circular or semi-elliptical, above the head of a door giving light to the hall.

Fenestration
The character and arrangement of windows in a building.

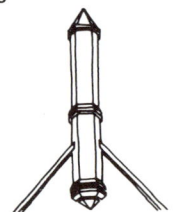

Finial
An ornamental feature at the top of a building or part of a building.

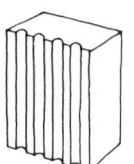

Fluting
The vertical grooves on the shaft of a column, pilaster or other surface.

Frieze
Properly the middle part of an entablature (q.v.). More generally a decorated band of masonry or plasterwork, usually just below a cornice.

Gable
The triangular end-wall of a building, usually supporting the roof.

Gargoyle
A projecting rainwater-spout, often decoratively treated in the form of a grotesque animal or human head.

Gibbsian Surround
The framing of a door in which the architrave (embracing the fanlight in the Kilkenny context) is interrupted by blocks set quoin-wise.

Glazing-bars
The divisions, usually of timber, between the small panes of a sash window (q.v.).

Glebe House
A house built as a residence for Church of Ireland clergymen (mostly between the 1770s and the 1830s).

Gothic
The style which began in the 13th Century, most easily recognised by the use of pointed arches, pinnacles, buttresses, etc. Revived in the 19th Century. See under Hard-Gothic.

Gothick
Light-hearted and half-hearted superficial imitation of Gothic details in work of the late 18th and early 19th Centuries. After 1840 it is superseded by Hard-Gothic (q.v.).

Hard-Gothic
A manner of building, especially of churches and public buildings, during the second half of the 19th Century, in which a serious attempt was made to reproduce the spirit and the details of mediaeval Gothic building.

Hiberno-Romanesque
The Irish round arched style used before the Anglo-Norman invasion, or a modern imitation of it.

Hipped, Half-hipped
See Roof.

Hood Mould (or Dripstone)
A projecting moulding over a door or window to throw off rain-water.

Ionic
One of the three Orders (q.v.) of classical architecture, in which spiral features (called volutes) project from the capital. The column shaft is usually fluted.

Lancet
A tall, narrow window, usually with a pointed head, found in Gothic architecture.

Lantern
A hollow glassed-in feature usually straddling the ridge of a roof. Usually octagonal, hexagonal or circular.

Light
A term denoting the separate openings of a window, or the openings on either side of a door. Shown above is a two-light window.

Lintel
The head of an opening when formed of a single piece of stone or timber. If built up of wedge-shaped stones or bricks it is a flat arch.

Loop
A small opening through which to fire an arrow, etc.

Lunette
A semi-circular opening.

Machicolation
A gallery or parapet projecting on brackets, built on the outside of castle walls or towers, with openings in the floor for defensive purposes. Also copied in the 19th Century for decorative effect.

Mausoleum
A monumental above-ground building of sepulchral purpose, usually in a graveyard.

Modillions
Properly, a small projecting console (q.v) supporting the upper part of a Corinthian or Composite cornice (q.v.) (but, loosely, any cornice).

Mullion
A vertical post of stone or timber dividing a window into two or more lights (q.v.).

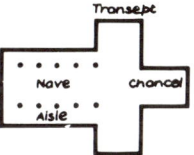

Nave
The principal space in a church.

Niche
A recess in a wall, usually semi-circular and arched. Niche porch: a recess containing a doorway.

Oculus
A circular window.

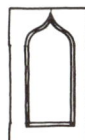

Ogee
A pointed arch made up of two S-curves.

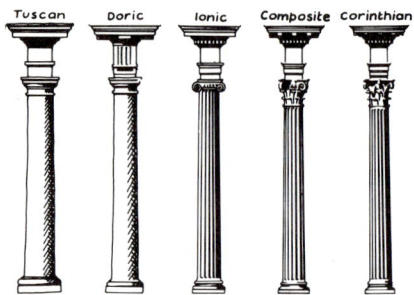

Order

A system of organisation, a grammar of architecture, evolved by the Greeks and used by the Romans, which is the basis of all classical architecture. In a complete order is a pedestal (if used), column with base, shaft and capital, an entablature with architrave, frieze and cornice. The size and proportion of these components vary with each order.

Oriel
A projecting window above ground level.

Oversailing Course
Courses of stone or brick where each course projects beyond the one beneath.

Parapet
A low protective wall on a bridge, at the edge of a quay, or above the cornice of a building.

Patera
An oval or circular ornament in classical architecture. Usually in low relief.

Pedestal
In general, a rectangular block supporting something. More especially, the block which may support the base of a column.

Pediment
A low-pitched triangular feature sometimes found over a portico (q.v.), a window-case, a door-case, etc. Broken-bed Pediment: when the base of the triangle is left open. Segmental pediment: when the "sides" form the segment of a circle.

Pier
A solid masonry support, usually square in section.

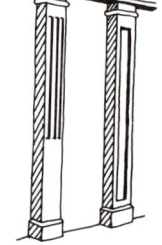

Pilaster
A shallow pier or rectangular column projecting only slightly from a wall. Shown above left, a fluted pilaster, and right, a hollow pilaster.

Plinth
The projecting base of a wall or pedestal.

Portico
A roofed space forming the entrance to a building.

Quatrefoil
Made up of four lobes.

Quoins
Regular stones at the corners of a building for strength and appearance, often rusticated (q.v.).

Relieving Arch
An arch built into a wall for the purpose of taking the major load off a lintel or arch below it.

Rendered
A general term for all forms of external plastering, whether lime-plaster (the traditional Irish way), Roman cement (early 19th Century), or Portland cement (the modern Irish way).

Return
The part of a wall or cornice etc, which runs back (usually at right angles) from the front of a structure.

Romanesque
The round-arched style of the 12th Century.

Roof
A cover over a building. Hipped roof: sloping rather than vertical gable ends. Half hipped: the ends are partly gabled and partly sloping.

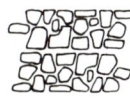 

Rubble Masonry
Walls of random undressed stones. Coursed rubble: the stones are roughly dressed and built in regular layers or courses. Snecked rubble: dressed stones varying in size with small rectangular fillings or snecks between them. Shown above: left, coursed: right, snecked.

 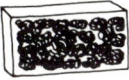

Rustication
The emphasising of individual blocks, or courses of stone, in masonry by deeply recessed joints and/or a roughened surface. See Ashlar for illustration of banded, chamfered and channelled rustication. Rock faced: stones irregularly surfaced to appear unfinished. Vermiculated: stone carved to give a worm-cast appearance. Shown above: left, rock faced: right, vermiculated.

Sanctuary
The part of the church around the altar.

Sash-window
A window in which the parts slide up and down. For illustration, see Aedicule.

Side-lights
Windows, usually narrow, flanking a doorway.

Sill
A horizontal slab beneath a window-frame to cast off the water.

Spur Stone (or Wheelguard)
A dressed stone at the corner of a building to protect the wall from damage by the hubs of carts.

String Course
A slightly projecting band of masonry or brickwork running across the facade of a building.

Tracery
The system of ribs, mullions, etc, locating and supporting the glass in mediaeval windows. Switch line tracery: resembling diverging railway lines. Perpendicular tracery: the mullions pass uninterrupted vertically to the head of the arch.

Transept
The part of a church lying at right angles to the nave (q.v.) and making it into a cruciform shape.

Transom
A horizontal bar dividing the upper from the lower parts of a window, or dividing a door from a fanlight.

Trefoil
Having 3 lobes — like a shamrock.

Vault
An arched construction, usually of brick or masonry.

Vermiculation
See Rustication.

Vernacular
The kind of building carried out by anonymous builders and craftsmen at any time down to the advent of prefabricated components, e.g. steel framed windows. The style is often governed by the use of local building materials.

Volute
A spiral ornament as found on, for example, an Ionic capital (see Order).

Voussoirs
The stones, or bricks, which form an arch or vault.

Weather slating
A method of protecting a wall from driving rain by nailing slates to it in overlapping courses.

Bibliographical References

References for further study are given below and are abbreviated as follows:

Carrigan
Carrigan, Rev William, The History and Antiquities of the Diocese of Ossory. Sealy Bryers and Walker, Dublin (1905) 4 vols.

Hogan
Hogan, John, Kilkenny. P. M. Egan, Kilkenny (1884).

J.R.S.A.I.
Journal of the Royal Society of Antiquaries of Ireland. Early numbers were known as the Journal of Kilkenny Archaeological Society and refer to the 1st Kilkenny Archaeological Society of 1849.

O.K.R.
Old Kilkenny Review. The Journal of the second Kilkenny Archaeological Society; published annually in Kilkenny since 1945.

I.G.S.J.
Irish Georgian Society Journal.

GENERAL HISTORICAL OUTLINE

The Pre-Norman Settlement
Roche, R, The Norman Invasion of Ireland, Anvil Books (1970): Carrigan, Vol III.

The Rise of the Feudal Families
Liber Primus Kilkenniensis, trans. Otway-Ruthven, Tholsel Archives.

The Kyteler Case
Harl Ms 641 Brit Mus, Trans. Ossory Arch Soc, (Morrin), Vol I, p 213: Clyn and Dowling, Annals of Ireland, Ed. Butler, Irish Arch Soc Dublin (1849): Carrigan, Vol I, p 49; Vol III, p 102: Ware, Archbishops and Bishops of Ireland, Dublin (1801), p 408: Leslie, Ossory Clergy and Parishes, Enniskillen (1938), p 6: Hogan, p 253: Walsh, R. A. Kytelers Inn, privately published (1966).

The Butlers
Dunboyne, Lord, Butler Family History, privately published (1967).

The 18th Century
'The Clasped Book', Kilkenny Corporation Archives: J.R.S.A.I, VII, 1862-63, p 154: Sparks and Bligh, Kilkenny, Kilkenny People (1926).

The 20th Century
Butler, H, The Kilkenny Theatre, O.K.R. No 3 (1950), p 24: J.R.S.A.I. Vol XXII, (1902), p 436: Files of Kilkenny Journal: Files of Kilkenny Moderator: Lanigan, K. M, Banim Brothers, O.K.R, No 25 (1973): McAdams, J. L, Ellen, Countess of Desart and Capt Otway Cuffe, (1958).

SECTION 1

Kilkenny Castle
Coll. Ormonde Deeds, National Library: Curtis, Calendar of Ormonde Deeds (1935): Carte, Life of Ormonde (1935: Calender of MSS of Ormonde, Historical MSS Commission, HMSO London, Vols I-VIII, (1902-20): Dunboyne, Lord Butler Family History, (1967): J.R.S.A.I, Vol II (1852-53), p 115: Folly, O.K.R, Vol I, No 2 (1975), p 103: Kenealy, O.K.R, No 22 (1970), p 44: Butler, O.K.R, No 3 (1950), p 24: Lanigan, K. M, Kilkenny Castle (1966): Smithwick, P, I.G.S.J., (Oct-Dec 1963): Curran, C. P, Irish Times, (9/5/67): Unpublished letters, Mrs Violette Sparrow.

The Shee Alms House
Kilkenny Journal, (14/9/1896): ibid, (24/2/1897): Poer-O'Shee Papers, Anal. Hib, No 20 (1958): J.R.S.A.I, Vol III, Parts 3 and 4, (1886): Healy, History of Kilkenny (1893).

St Mary's Church and Graveyard
Carrigan, Vol III, p 90: O.K.R, No 17 (1965), p 18: Phelan and Buggy, Tombs of St Mary's, Rothe House Library.

Rothe House
Lanigan, K. M, 'Rothe House', K.A.S. (1966): Lanigan, K. M, O.K.R, No 15, (1963), p 30: Hurley, O.K.R, No 17 (1965), p 19: Johnson, O.K.R, No 21 (1969), p 51: Petrie, O.K.R, No 20 (1968), p 45: Harbison, O.K.R, No 25 (1973), p 34.

St Francis Abbey
Carrigan, Vol I, p 45: ibid, Vol III, p 104: Conlon, O.K.R, Vol I, No 2, (1975): Clyn and Dowling Annals, Ed. Butler, Dublin (1849).

The Black Abbey
Fenning et al, Black Abbey, (1975): J.R.S.A.I, (1851, 1865, 1947): Carrigan, Vol III: Gaffney, O.K.R, No 17, (1965): Roe, Helen, O.K.R, No 24 (1972).

St Canice's Cathedral
Graves and Prim, Hist. of the Cathedral Church of St Canice, (1857): Stalley, C, Architecture and Sculpture in Ireland: Hunt, John, Irish Mediaeval Figure Sculpture, London (1947): Rae, E. C, J.R.S.A.I, Vol 100 Part 1, (1970): ibid, Vol 10, part 1, (1971): Kenealy, O.K.R, Vol 5, No 1, (1974), p 26: Gibb, O.K.R, No 6 (1953) p 50: Rae, E. C, O.K.R, No 18, p 62, (1966).

St Canice's Library
Woodward, O.K.R, No 22, p 5: ibid, No 23, p 15: Jackson, O.K.R, No 17.

The Bishop's Palace
Smithwick, P, Georgian Kilkenny, I.G.S.J, (Oct-Dec 1963), p 75.

The Priory of St John the Evangelist
Carrigan, Vol III, p 241: Tombs of St Johns Priory, Rothe House Library.

SECTION 2

Kenny's Well
Fenning et al, 750 Years of the Black Abbey, (1975), p 3.

Talbot's Castle and City Wall
Kenealy, O.K.R, No 2, (1948), p 32: Birthistle, O.K.R, No 18, (1966), p 5: Bradley, O.K.R, Vol I, No 2, (1975) p 85: Bradley, O.K.R, Vol I, No 3, (1976), p 209.

The Slips
Kilkenny Corporation Documents.

Tudor Kilkenny
Kenealy, O.K.R, No 5, (1952), p 5: Murphy, O.K.R, No 7, (1954), p 1: Phelan, O.K.R, Nos 6, 7, 12, 13 and 20: Prim, J.R.S.A.I, Vol VII, p 169.

Georgian Kilkenny
Smithwick, P, I.G.S.J, (Oct-Dec 1963): Bligh, O.K.R, No 15, (1963), p 43.

Kilkenny Writers
The Kilkenny Magazine, No 1, (Summer 1960), p 3: ibid, No 7, (Summer 1962), p 49: ibid, No 10, (Autumn-Winter 1963-64), p 35: Escarbelt, B, Introduction to 'The Boyne Water', C.E.R.I.U.L, Lille, (1976).

SECTION 3

The Parade
No 4: Butler, O.K.R, No 3, p 24: Butler, O.K.R, No 22, p 48: Clark, W. Smith, The Irish Stage in Country Towns. **No 10:** Smithwick, P, I.G.S.J, (Oct-Dec 1963). **East Side:** Society Minutes, K.S.P.C.A.

Castle Road
St James Asylum: Smithwick, P, I.G.S.J, (Oct-Dec 1963).

Patrick Street
Kenealy, O.K.R, No 15, p 5: Kenealy, O.K.R, No 16, p 33. **Nos 7 and 8:** Murphy, C, O.K.R, No 2, p 48. **Butler House:** Phelan, Journal of the Butler Society, No 4, p 236. **Kilkenny Theatre:** McAdams, J. L, Ellen Countess of Desart and Capt Otway Cuffe, (1958): O'Sullivan, D, Irish Times, (9/10/64). **Nos 33 and 34:** Kenealy, O.K.R, No 15, (1963): Kenealy, O.K.R, No 16, (1964): Smithwick, P, I.G.S.J, (Oct-Dec 1963).

Ormonde Road
Technical School: Atkinson, Donald H, The Irish Education Experiment, Routledge & Keegan, (1970).

College Road
St Kieran's College: Birch, Rev P, St Kieran's College, Gill, Dublin, (1951). **Rose Hill Hotel:** Parliamentary Papers, 1808 (205) XIII, p 167: Neale, J. P, Views of the Seats, Vol 6, (1823): Kilkenny City Presentments, (1830), P.R.O, Dublin : Robertson, Wm, Diary 1795-1797, Nat Lib, Dublin: Robertson, J. G, Antiquities and Scenery of Co. Kilkenny, T. Shearman, printer, Kilkenny, (1851): Quarterly Bulletin, Irish Georgian Society, Vol XV, (1970).

Rose Inn Street
De Loughrey, O.K.R, No 18, p 9: Sparks, M, and Bligh, E, Inns and Taverns of Old Kilkenny, Kilkenny People.

High Street
Phelan, M, and Lanigan, K, O.K.R, No 6: Phelan, M, O.K.R. Nos 7, 12, 13 and 20. **Nos 4 — 9:** Birthistle, Alms Houses of Kilkenny, O.K.R, No 16. **The Hole in the Wall:** J.R.S.A.I, Vol VII, (1862-3), p 169. **Nos 17 — 19:** Kenealy, O.K.R, No 5. **The Tholsel:** Bligh, Corporation Regalia, O.K.R, No 17, p 67: Phelan, O.K.R, No 2, p 48. **Colles Family:** Murphy, O.K.R, No 2, (1948), p 14: Boate, Geology of Ireland, (1742): Fallon, Abraham Colles, Heinemann, (1972): Lyons, J. B, J.I. Medical Assoc, Vol 66, No 14, (July 1973), p 374. **Woolworth & Crotty:** Kenealy, O.K.R, No 5, p 35.

Detail Rothe Monument, St Canices 1642 AP

Pennefeather Lane
Capuchin Friary: Tercentenary of Capuchin Foundations in Kilkenny 1648-1948, Souvenir Booklet.

Chapel Lane & Wellington Square
Carrigan, Vol III, p 126: Birch, St Kieran's College, p 19.

James Street
St Mary's Cathedral: Phelan, M, O.K.R, No 24, p 4: Phelan, M, St Mary's Cathedral, (1972).

James Sconce
The Maltings: Smithwick, P, The Sullivans, O.K.R, No 16.

St Kieran Street
Kenealy, St Kieran Street, O.K.R, No 17. **Kytelers Inn:** Carrigan, Vol I, p 49: Carrigan, Vol III, p 102: Walsh, O.K.R, No 18, p 94: Lanigan, O.K.R, No 15, p 23.

Parliament Street
DeLoughrey, O.K.R, No 3. **The Courthouse:** The Sheffield Grace Memoirs: Rocques Map, Survey of City of Kilkenny (1758): Finns Leinster Journal, (Kilkenny Journal Files): Proceedings of the Royal Archaeological Society, (1874/5), p 318: Sparks, O.K.R, No 19.

Dean Street
St Canices's Widow Asylum: Carrigan, Vol III, p 207.

Butts Green
Cross: Hogan, pp 155-157: ibid, p 362: Carrigan, Vol III, p 191: J.R.S.A.I, (1853).

Blackmill Street
No 38: DeLoughrey, James Stephens.

The Coach Road and Church Lane
Graves & Prim, History and Antiquities of St Canice's Cathedral. **The Deanery:** Hogan, p 346: Carrigan, Vol III, p 174. **Loreto Convent:** Birch, Dr P, St Kieran's College.

Troy's Gate
Phelan and Gibb, O.K.R, No 9.

John's Quay
No 3: Phelan, O.K.R, No 10, (1958).

John Street Lower
Finn & Murphy, O.K.R, No 14, p 25. **Evans Poor House:** Carrigan, Vol III, p 255: Egan, Guide and Directory 1895, p 262. **Kilkenny College:** Smithwick, P, I.G.S.J, (Oct-Dec 1963): Browne, J.R.S.A.I, Vol I, Part 2, (1850), p 221: Dobbs, W. F, Kilkenny College, (1938).

Maudlin Street
Magdalen Tower: Corporation Records, Town Hall: Carrigan, Vol III, p 248: O.K.R, No 21.

Dublin Road
Wind Gap Cottage: Lanigan, Banim in Wind Gap Cottage, O.K.R, No 3. **St John's Graveyard:** Clohosey, St John's Graveyard (record of grave slabs): Clohosey, O.K.R, No 13: Lanigan, O.K.R, No 13. **St John's Church:** McAdams, Count Thomas O'Loughlin, O.K.R, Vol I, No 2.